The High Calling:
Life Worth Living

Philippians 3: 14 I press toward the goal to the prize
of the high calling of God in Christ Jesus.

Chris A. Legebow

ISBN-978-0-9952715-3-1

DEDICATION

I thank God for the Apostles, Prophets, Evangelists, Pastors and Teachers who have taught me. I thank God for the churches I have been a part of. I thank God for the Macchiavello family. I thank God for those who have invested in my life spiritually by training and mentoring me. I thank God for Christian media especially GloryStar and TBN for giving me Christian connections that inspired and enriched me. I have been given much of God's Word; I received much excellent teaching and preaching. I thank God for Joyce Meyer and Kenneth and Gloria Copeland and International House of Prayer Kansas City. There is a list of preachers and teachers too numerous to record here. I thank God for them because they impacted my life with God's truth.

CONTENTS

ACKNOWLEDGMENTS

All Scriptures taken from Bible Gateway.com
Modern English Version (MEV)

INTRODUCTION

This book is written to teenagers, twenty somethings, thirty somethings and anyone who want to inherit the promises of God. It is a book about the importance of learning all you can from those in spiritual authority in your life. It is about giving to those around you including the generation that follows you. It is about giving yourself wholly to God that God might use you to be a vessel He can use. God wants to use you; you are unique. You are special and there is no one else who can reach people in your life the way you can do.

Even if things are rough, because of finances or other things, because we live in a fallen world and because not all people have perfect families or homes, you must put your trust in God and His Word. God is always faithful. The way through life is going through dressed in the armour of God with the high praise of God in the mouth and in your spirit and a two-edged sword in your hand (Psalm 149). The way to live is to pass through valleys not to stay there. Through God's Spirit in you, faith in His Word, the blood of Jesus and giving your life wholly to Jesus, you can overcome all obstacles.

Learn all you can from mentors and connect with peers. Live in the high calling of God in Christ Jesus for your life. Sow to the Spirit that you might reap of the Spirit. That means make investments in your own life spiritually; get all the preaching, teaching, books cd's etc. you can to build up yourself. Be encouraged to press into God with all your life's being and to never stop pressing in to God. Live holy and wholly for God every day of your life giving your best unto Him. Do it every day of your life for all the days of your life. Influence as many people for Christ as you can.

All members of the Body of Christ are important and that you are a vital member in the body. You are living your high calling when you are giving yourself, wholly, holy unto God: spirit, soul, and body (1 Thessalonians 5: 23). Your spiritual gifts are important for you to use but they are also important for you to use in the local church so that the local body of Christ can receive the fullness of the Spirit of God flowing through all the members. This cause the glory of God to be seen in the Church.

First, the high calling of God, next the Joshua anointing to inherit the promises of God, next being an overcomer and sowing to the Spirit and Living in the high calling of God in Christ Jesus and finally all members of the Body of Christ are important.

Chris Legebow

1. THE HIGH CALLING OF GOD

The high calling of God is God's purposes for your life to be known by you. It is living on the earth but not of the earth. It will include prayer, Bible study, service, giving and wholly following God. The advantages that come from it are too numerous to list. If you are single, seek God with all your being.

Do not think that if you marry a believer with the same values you are doing something that isn't the best. If you are equally yoked, with someone who loves God with the same fervency and passion, you can both serve the LORD together as well as have some separate ministries. Usually, Christian marriage is for children to be raised as Christians but also for couples to minister as a team. This is not less of the will of God. You will find your place by seeking God first.

If you seek marriage first, you may choose someone because you don't want to be alone. You may choose someone who is not equally yoked. You may be lead astray. If you seek a career first, you may become covetous. You may become power driven rather than Spirit lead. Please see, it makes the most sense for you to seek God first while you can with your whole heart. It will be as a trampoline that propels you into the best God has for your life. You will aligned with people of like precious faith. You will develop spiritual fruit and joy and prosperity. You will be aligned with the right kind of people. You will position yourself in a place where God can bless you with the best because you are giving your all to Him.

You may become a plumber or a teacher or a bus driver, a factory worker or a manager. Your life career is really a very important part of your life. God wants to use you in that place to shine the light of Christ. Whatever your education or job, God wants to use you. I, because I am a teacher and by my life's experience, will always encourage you to get a diploma or a degree or both. The more education you get, the more opportunities become available to you. God can use you in a different capacity to reach different people.

God can use you, whatever your education or your profession to speak His word, to pray for people, to sow light into the earth. I literally mean your godly character shines brightly because you are living as a vessel of honour. I mean you choose the high way, the high call of God, the way of the Holy Spirit. That means you live your life with excellence and integrity. You give your best. You are responsible. You are trustworthy. It means all your life is a reflection of God's Spirit living in you and through you. You will be able to witness for Christ because people see the fruit of your life. They realize that you love God but that you show excellence in all aspects of life. It will make your witness more effective because they see the fruit of God's blessing on you in your excellence of character and of lifestyle. You will be able to invite people to church and they may come because of you. You will have a point of connection to all the people in the spheres of authority of your life because you have spiritual fruit such as patience, meekness, temperance, forbearance, peace, joy, humility, mercy, compassion, love, etc. (Galatians 5).

Press into God First

The High call of God is the most excellent way because it is a way of living a holy life as an example to others as you pursue Jesus Christ with all your being. Although all Christians are called to this excellent life, at some point in their lives, not all choose it. It doesn't mean you might not get to heaven. If you believe in Jesus Christ and His blood shed for you, that alone is your way to heaven. What it means if you choose not the way of Spirit – the way of pursuing God with all your life's energy, is that you will live below your calling. This is what it might mean.

You might not marry the best possible person, because you did not pursue God first. You might not get the best job possible, because you didn't get all the education you could. It might mean you might not get the things you desire as important such as a large home or car etc. It might mean, you do not meet the best possible friends for your life, because you were not at the right place to meet them. Please see what is directly affected is your life on earth, and with it your ability to impact the earth for Christ at your best level.

Yes, you can have as much of God as you want. You do not have to press in for the best that God has for you. The temporary easier way is not the best way. Usually, you must apply yourself 100 % to knowing God to meet the right people, to know what career you should get and to know the friends you should be with. Put God first as long as you live. Especially to you who are wanting to know your place in the earth, press into God first and you will find it.

You can have as much of Jesus as you want. As you press in, keep pressing and don't stop. Along the way you will meet the right people, make the right choices, find the best jobs etc. You will be used by God to witness to people all along your way. God will place people in your life that you can build up and encourage and teach. God can share His heart with you concerning your nation, your province or state or your city; your church or your family or your friends. God can speak to you in the place of communion with Him where you will clearly know God's will for you and you will be used to share Christ and encourage people with scripture as you do.

Do You Want More?

One of the sort of privileges we in North America take for granted is " more". In 2/3 of the earth the people scrounge for food and daily needs. We in North America, and Western Society make decisions such as, "should I have seconds?" Please see we are so privileged in live in a democracy where we can pursue education and career of our choosing. We can marry or remain single, of our choosing. In many countries these things are determined by others. There are countries where Christians have to meet in secret caves or basements to worship God or read the Bible. There are places where the Bible is forbidden and Christians are killed if caught worshipping or sharing Christ with others. I say this only to remind you, God has given you a special gift if you are living in the western world – the free world of democracy.

You can serve God with all your being and you can do it with others in a church building. If you want to, you can buy Bibles and give them as presents. Please recognize the special gift you have in our free nation. In some countries they hide their Bibles for fear of losing them or losing their lives because of them. You can serve your God. The only hindrance is you should you decide not to. If you are in a position to give yourself to God – do it with all your being. Live for God pursuing His best for you so that you can not only get the best of life for yourself and your family but also so God can use you as a living witness of His glory.

You never learn the Word of God for your own self only. You do it so you can share with others and teach others. It could be to share with family members, or your children or your friends. Most often, God will use us to share with the people in our lives. Whatever we get from God is not to keep alone. The Word of God you share can reach the people in your life like from no other person. You can impart to people in your church; it could be to impart to strangers you may meet that day. The Word of God is always for you to sow into others' lives as well as your own. You might write the scripture on a card and send it to someone. You could write books. Pray and ask God to use you; fill yourself with God's Word and start sowing the Word into others.

How to Start Sowing the Word of God on Purpose

Speak the scripture to someone at church. Write a tweet or a Face Book post with a scripture. Start a Blog. It isn't hard and what you would be doing directly is sowing God's Word into a place where others could be built up and encouraged by it. Post it so somebody could see how is expressing Himself to you and through you. You could do a UTube video of something Christ has put on your heart or some testimony to encourage others. Writing encouraging cards to shut ins or people ill or bereaved is an excellent way to directly build up the body of Christ.

If you are receiving but not giving, it is not right. God wants you to sow into others. Matthew 10:8b "Freely you have received, freely give." The gospel is for all the people of the earth, all ages, ethnicities, people groups etc. It's what we should be doing, sowing the Word of God into others as long as we live or until Jesus comes. You don't have to be a preacher to share what God has done for you. Tell how God answered your prayers, how He encouraged you, how He taught you. What you will be doing is giving God glory and building up someone else in the faith.

Legacy in the Earth

The more you share what God has done for you, the more you give God glory. What you impart to others of the Spirit is your legacy in the earth. It is wise to leave an inheritance of finances, possessions, things to your children and family. How much more important is to leave a spiritual legacy of what God has done for you. You do it by telling your story, how you were saved, how God drew you to Himself, how He provided for you, how He answered your prayers, how He healed you. You should be imparting these things to your children, grandchildren, family members and friends. Someone close to you should know how God delivered you or healed you. If you don't know what else to do – and don't see your family, start posting it on the Internet.

God wants to use you in the earth. That is the reason you were born. That is the reason He created you.. In my own life, I know it was a total miracle that God could reach me because I wanted God but I was completely away from God into other pagan gods and the occult – the wrong way. If God had mercy on me and reached me, I know He can reach people who are not serving Him. Your testimony is a way to give God glory.

The People Closest to you

If you living with your parents or your spouse and children, you should be sharing what God is doing for you with them. You should be sowing scripture into their lives in some practical way. As you are gathered as a family, always honour the LORD by reading a scripture and praying togther. It doesn't have to be long always; you can do it as the LORD leads you but you should be doing it.

Sowing into your family

I know families where the mom and dad or mom or dad pray for their kids each day before they go to school. They lay hands and say a prayer over their kids for protection and safety. They also do the same thing each evening before the kids go to bed. Some families home school their children so the Word of God is taught as the top priority. I realize not all parents can do it all; I also know some homes are single parent families so it is extremely tough, but you pray and ask God to show you how to sow the Word of God into your kids' lives. He will do it.

Sow into Your Friends and Associates

Sometimes, I have done this and it is if a particular book has blessed me, I buy several copies of it and sow it into people's lives prayerfully. I am directly supporting a Christian Ministry by doing it and I am connecting people who might not know about the blessings of that ministry. By doing this giving, you are a double blessing. Certainly, it is a way to minister if you yourself cannot speak with the people at length. If a CD or DVD has blessed you, share it or buy extra copies of it for someone in your life. Buy the materials; pray over them and give them praying for the people believing that God wants to reach others with the truths you have learned. Pray that God will use you to sow the Word of God into people's lives to enrich their spiritual life. Your sowing God's Word into people is a special way for you to sow to the Spirit that you might leave a legacy of faith in the earth.

Gather in your Church

You must be part of a local church where you can worship and praise with other Christians and serve and give and grow. If you do not have a Church like this, search and pray that God will lead you to one. The local church is the place where most of our daily life is covered: children are dedicated; people are baptized; people are baptized in the Holy Spirit; people are married; people are buried. It is a place where the preacher feeds you and not only you but all the sheep receive something whether mature or new Christians. It is a place of gathering. It is best when you know the Church you are in feels like home. Most of my Christian life was that way. I could hardly wait to get to church because I knew it would be awesome. There would be praise and worship and the word would be especially from God for me. I thought all Christian life was like that. I didn't know it could be different.

Sometimes, you may be in a place that you require additional preaching and teaching to be spiritually built up. Do it and thank God for it. In North America, we have a wealth of ministries to choose from to get teaching and preaching. Go to a local church that is solid in teaching; don't wander from place to place. I've known people who stop going to church because they can't find a church that feeds them. Go to a church that preaches the Word of God as the truth. Even though it may not be perfect, it is a place where people that love Christ gather. I am saying don't stop going to church. I've known people who have bounced from church to church randomly wandering not knowing what to do so they stop trying. I have known others who become offended at someone and stop going. Please see this for what it truly is. It is an attack on you to try to cut you off from the Body of Christ.

If your Church Isn't Enough

It may be that you attend a Church that is less than your spiritual need. God can bless you there anyhow. God can use you and you might become part of the revival of the place. Should you get opportunity to join a dynamite church, take the opportunity and do it – at God's leading not by your wandering around. Pray about it seriously. The church you attend should believe the Word of God as the highest standard of life. The church should believe and flow in the gifts of the Spirit. There should be a strong integrity in the pastor or pastors. The church should honour Jesus. The praise and worship should make you want to praise and worship God. The preached word should be feeding your spirit. The people should want to praise and worship God. That should be the reason they gather together – to glorify the LORD Jesus Christ.

If these things are present in your church but you require supplements to feed yourself – do it. Keep going to Church, praying for God to revive the people. Keep being faithful in sowing and in serving. Please know there have been saints throughout Biblical History who have either been alone or been in places of temporary provision. You may be in a place of temporary provision. That means you be faithful on your part and believe God for a more permanent provision but also it means you contribute and pray that God will teach you and show you how to be a blessing while you are there.

Avoid Strife

If someone at church has offended you by a word or comment or behaviour, you should go to the person and speak to him or her privately explaining it. The person may not even know he or she has offended you. The person may repent right there and you will pray and God can heal it. If the person is willfully offending you and will not repent, get an elder or pastor to meet with you and the person. The person can understand how serious the offense was and repent.

If the person still continues, he or she may be cut off from the congregation because of it. Please know it is rare that these things are done. Rarely does a person who has been offended confront the person. Do it with a meek and gentle spirit. The other alternative is to let it bounce off you. Get some thick skin so that you realize a demon is using that person to try to offend you. Refuse to be offended.

If you have offended someone, repent immediately. Say it to the person. Ask for forgiveness. Proverbs 18: 21 "Death and life are in the power of the tongue, and those who love it will eat its fruit.." Pray for the Holy Spirit to lead you into praying for the person so that he or she can be healed. Realize that offenses can deeply wound someone. Whether you intended to offend the person (probably not) or did it in ignorance, pray for God to heal the person and your relationship with that person.

Gatherers of the Lambs

We as Christians should pray for God to make us gatherers of the lambs and the sheep rather than offenders. We should know the people who we usually sit around and if any of them are missing, we should mention it to a leader or pastor. We should care for the sheep. This is not only for the pastors or the leaders in the church. It is also for you whether or not you have a spiritual title in the church. The parts of the body of Christ should care about and build up the other parts.

Galatians 6: 1 Brothers, if a man is caught in any transgression, you who are spiritual should restore such a one in the spirit of meekness, watching yourselves, lest you also be tempted. 2 Bear one another's burdens, and so fulfill the law of Christ. 3 For if someone thinks himself to be something when he is nothing, he deceives himself. 4 But let each one examine his own work, and then he will have rejoicing in himself alone, and not in another.

Should a friend or associate from Church, who you know, has become offended and stopped coming, or who has sinned and has stopped coming, pray that God might use you to restore such a person. Proverbs 11: 30 "The fruit of the righteous is a tree of life, and he who wins souls is wise." You must do it with meekness and humility. You must do it with gentleness and truth. If you are phony, they will spot you. Such opportunities are gathering opportunities. Rather than leave a lamb or sheep caught in the briar bush, do your best to speak with him or her and to reconcile the person to the church. This may mean getting two people together to talk to each other and pray together. Usually it means, sharing your heart and praying for the person and gently leading them in discussion, pray and return to the church. I don't know how often it happens. When it does happen, you don't brag about it. You do it with humility and you pray restoring that soul to the local church. Once restored, God can completely heal the person and cause him or her to grow.

James 5: 19 Brothers, if any one of you strays from the truth and someone corrects him, 20 let him know that he who converts the sinner from the error of his way will save a soul from death and will cover a multitude of sins.

It is not casual joining a church or leaving a church. Do it prayerfully. Should you find a different church that you feel you want to go to, approach your current pastor and ask him or her to pray a blessing for you as you go. A true shepherd will do it without selfish desire to keep you. A true shepherd knows that the sheep that belong will stay and the shat not all people stay at the same church all their lives. The right way to leave a church is to pray first yourself and with those close to you in spiritual relationship and then to ask the pastor to pray with you. God gives us a place whether permanent or temporary. We should honour God because of the spiritual covering over you.

Start Including Others

Part of what a leader does, is find ways to include others and help them to grow spiritually. If you are in youth group or a group of twenty somethings or whatever, invite someone new to join you. If you notice a new face, make friends, include them in prayer groups, group activities etc. This is a way for you to use the gift of encouragement and leadership simultaneously. Invite others to join you. It strengthens the church and makes a way for those people to connect with other Christians. If you are not currently serving in your church, start. If you get the opportunity to help clean, do dishes, serve tables, translate, teach, help with Sundays school, do it. Serving in the local church is surely something God wants you to do. You will be using your spiritual gifts. God can connect you with others. You will be building up the church. This is God's desire for each of us – that we would contribute to the local church.

Psalm 139: 1 O Lord, You have searched me
  and known me.
2 You know when I sit down and when I get up;
  You understand my thought from far off.
3 You search my path and my lying down
  and are aware of all my ways.
4 For there is not a word on my tongue,
  but behold, O Lord, You know it fully.
5 You put Yourself behind and before me,
  and keep Your hand on me.
6 Such knowledge is too wonderful for me;
  it is lofty, and I cannot fathom it.

7 Where shall I go from Your spirit,
  or where shall I flee from Your presence?
8 If I ascend to heaven, You are there;
  if I make my bed in Sheol, You are there.
9 If I take the wings of the morning
  and dwell at the end of the sea,
10 even there Your hand shall guide me,
  and Your right hand shall take hold of me.
11 If I say, "Surely the darkness shall cover me,
  and the light shall be as night about me,"
12 even the darkness is not dark to You,
  but the night shines as the day,
  for the darkness is like light to You.
13 You brought my inner parts into being;
  You wove me in my mother's womb.
14 I will praise you, for You made me with fear and wonder;
  marvelous are Your works,
  and You know me completely.
15 My frame was not hidden from You

when I was made in secret,
and intricately put together in the lowest parts of the earth.
16   Your eyes saw me unformed,
yet in Your book all my days were written, before any of them came into being

You are a Gift to Your Generation

This passage of scripture is the Psalmist writing about the LORD's knowing us before we were placed into our mother's womb on the earth. The revelation here is that God knew us and purposely gave us a physical body, parents, family etc. All of the aspects concerning your life were known by God and God chose to give you as a gift to your family and to the earth. God first created you in thought. You existed as a thought of God before the foundations of the earth. He chose your mother. He chose to knit within in you gifts and talents. You are a spirit; you have a soul (mind, will and emotions) and live in the body God gave to you. God placed your living spirit into your physical body.

Everyone does not know that he or she has a high calling of God in life. Some people believe only apostles, prophets, pastors, evangelists and teachers have a calling of God on their lives. It's true they do but so do you. You are a Christian, so God dwells in you. He wants to use your unique life qualities and opportunities so you can be an effective witness for Christ. Yes, it is true that you have certain main gifts and talents, but don't limit God. Should you be willing and obedient, He can use you in unusual ways to reach all sorts of people. Don't limit God thinking that He can't use you. Nothing in your past can prevent God from using you in the present.

1 John 1: 9 9 If we confess our sins, He is faithful and just to forgive us our sins and cleanse us from all unrighteousness.

Jesus blood can wash you as if you had never sinned. The Holy Spirit living on the inside of you can give you boldness to preach and teach Christ and to win souls. You can reach people others can't because of your unique qualities and character. Usually, there are three or four top motivational Spiritual gifts in a Spirit filled Christian, but God could use you in the other gifts if you were willing and obedient. If you were the only Christian in someone's life and there was a need for a gift to manifest, you could be the vessel God would use. You would first have to believe that God could and wanted to. You would have to totally rely on the Holy Spirit and give God all the glory.

I have known of people who God has used uniquely in a miraculous way to be an answer to someone's prayer. I myself have had God use me in different ways depending on the people or congregation I was in. If I had not been willing, or I had not obeyed, God could have used someone else and I would not have had the pleasure or the joy of being a co labourer with Christ in praying for people, laying hands on people, prophesying etc.

If you are Willing

God can use you if you are first willing. God will never force you to do anything. It is by your own free will that you pray something like "God please use me today." If you pray like that, expect God to place people in your life that you can minister to. Expect God to give you opportunities to shine the light of Christ by sharing Jesus with people and how God has answered prayer; how God has healed you or how God has delivered you; how God has made your life more joyful and given you a hopeful attitude. A simple prayer – add it to your day before you go out into the world: God use me. I would also recommend that as you grow spiritually, you pray stirring up the gifts of God and also reading scripture and asking God to let you sow it into people throughout the day.

Would you let God use you even if it took you out of your comfort zone? Let me give you an example of it. I am a teacher and I was on lunch break at a restaurant. I was alone and out for just a short bit before returning to school. I noticed the restaurant was packed with people. It was a fast food restaurant. A man and I assume his wife and a child were walking towards their seat and the man stumbled to the ground and lay there.

I saw it and thought perhaps he slipped. Within seconds, I saw he wasn't moving. I rushed over to the man and asked permission of his wife to pray for him. She said "Yes. Please". I kneeled. I knew the Holy Spirit had moved me. I prayed the healing power of Christ to fill that man's body. I prayed he would gain strength and totally be healthy. People around me were gathering and the restaurant manager had phoned for an ambulance. I knew that God was using me. Within a minute or two, the man moved and sat up. He sat at the table and had lunch with his family. I did not stay. I did not preach a sermon. I left the restaurant knowing God had used me. It wasn't because I have the healing gifts especially strong or because I was so anointed. Yes. God anointed me – but it was because I was willing and I was obedient. A big part of God using you is that if He prompts your heart, you are willing to obey.

I can't remember the day I started praying it, but at some early point in my Christian life as a new Christian, I started praying for God to use me. I wanted to share the goodness of Christ with others. I wanted people to know that Jesus is real. God has given me special opportunities to reach strangers that I have only encountered briefly such as what I described above. These were divine connections. There was a need for intervention, I was there. I was willing. I gave myself to God. The Holy Spirit directed me to pray or prophesy or witness to someone. Start praying that God will use you. Believe that because our God is so awesome, He can use you to minister as Jesus would. The first thing to do is offer yourself to Jesus as a vessel He can use.

If you truly know that Jesus Christ has radically changed your life and given you joy, peace, abundance, prosperity, etc. You will want to share it with others. Don't think God can't or won't if you give yourself to Him sincerely. God wants to use you to tell others about Him.

Romans 10: 14 How then shall they call on Him in whom they have not believed? And how shall they believe in Him of whom they have not heard? And how shall they hear without a preacher? 15 And how shall they preach unless they are sent? As it is written: "How beautiful are the feet of those who preach the gospel of peace, who bring good news of good things!"

Obedience

For God to use you, you must be obedient also. It is good to be willing but you have got to know the promptings of the Holy Spirit and obey them. There have been situations where I felt the LORD prompting me to speak to a person or do something for someone. It is like a brief prompt. I recognize the source as God. You have a choice. Obey or ignore it. Each opportunity I have obeyed the LORD there has been a mighty result. Pray for Spiritual discernment that you might know what the LORD is prompting you to do.

I remember one occasion I was praying at church with all the leaders and teachers of the Vacation Bible school that was to start the next week. I was at the altar and the presence of God was so strong in that place because we were believing for kids to be saved, baptized in the Holy Spirit etc. I was so overwhelmed with the presence of God I was high on God. I have learned that when this occurs I should pray for God to use me. I did. I was singing in the spirit driving home (a 1 hour drive) offering myself to God. I saw a car pulled over on the side of the left side of the highway (not the best spot) the lights were flashing. I felt God prompt me to stop. Listen, late at night in a large city, single women don't stop to help motorists. It isn't logical. I don't know much about auto mechanics. How could I help? All those things flashed through my spirit in response to God's prompting.

I heard God Say " Pull over and help her." I knew it was God. I stopped, pulled over. I was not sure it was a woman – but for the voice of God. I stopped. There was a woman in her 40;s sitting in the driver's seat in her pajamas drinking beer and as drunk as a skunk. She was in no position to drive. Anyone who came along could take advantage of her easily.

As soon as I saw her I said " God told me to help you." She was drunk and started crying " I was praying for a miracle!" As I helped her she started pouring out her life story to me. I assessed the situation coolly and realized her radiator had over heated. I always drank pop and kept the bottles for refund in my trunk. God gave me a clear logical plan to help this woman. I told her to come with me. I didn't let her come in the store. She was in her pajamas! I filled all the bottles with water. We drove to her car and I refilled the water. I believe I also bought some temporary fluid for radiators. That was the logical part. I knew she shouldn't be driving, but I told her to drive home and I would follow her with my car. I followed her several miles out of my way until she was safe in her apartment building.

She poured out horrible things of her life like divorce, boyfriends, her daughter who was ill… it was like she was telling me everything about her life. I let her talk a long while. At one point I told her to stop and I told her that God loved her so much that He prompted me to stop for her. I prayed the sinners prayer with her. I plead the blood over her. I went home later than usual knowing God did use me to help someone that I normally wouldn't even see. I obeyed the prompting. What if you don't obey? God can use someone else or the person will not receive help. Obedience is the main thing.

2 JOSHUA ANOINTING: INHERITING THE PROMISES

Joshua 1: 1 Now after the death of Moses the servant of the Lord, the Lord spoke to Joshua son of Nun, the assistant of Moses: 2 "Moses My servant is dead, so now get up and cross over the Jordan—you and all this people—to the land that I am giving to the children of Israel.

This passage of scripture is quite familiar to most Christians as preachers constantly refer to them. It is an important passage because it is the inheriting of the promise of God to Israel for the land of Israel promised by God to Abraham, Isaac and Jacob and finally to Moses and Joshua. Because of the sin of unbelief, the Israelites wandered in the wilderness for 40 years. They did not receive the good report that Joshua. and Caleb had brought believing that God could give them the promised land.

Because of their unbelief, Israel was not allowed to go in to the land of promise until all the people who didn't believe died. God provided for them; God kept them and protected them but they could not receive the promise. Unbelief is sin and it separates you from God; it can also separate you from the promises of God or blessings that God wants to release to you.

Joshua Served God by Serving Moses

After those 40 years of wandering, Joshua is about to lead Israel into Canaan land. It was this same Joshua who faithfully served Moses all those years, learning whatever he could as he respected and faithfully obeyed Moses as a servant of God. Moses had returned to Egypt upon God's command that he go speak to Pharaoh (the leader of Egypt) and tell him to let the Israelite slaves go free. This command seemed ridiculous to Pharaoh and his heart was hard and refused to let Israel go free. After the plagues, culminating with the death of the 1st born of all the inhabitants of Egypt including Pharaoh's son, Pharaoh let the Israelites go free. This is a miraculous event. Israel had been slaves to Egypt for 400 years. Only God could release Israel from such a situation.

Eye Witness to the Miracles

Joshua had been an eye witness to the miracles God did. Joshua had seen Moses faithfully obey God and served willingly to help Moses. Throughout the book of Exodus and Deuteronomy (books on the deliverance of Israel) Joshua is mentioned as one of the wise elders and one of the 12 spies who believed God would give Israel the land that was promised. Only Joshua and Caleb believed God's promise. The other spies doubted God and spoke words that caused Israel to fear, doubt God and turn on Moses.

If Israel had believed Joshua and Caleb's report that God would give them the promised land, they would not have wandered through the wilderness. They would have obtained their promise within a week or so. Because of the sin of unbelief in God, Israel was sentenced to wander for forty years. The spies who spoke a negative fearful report magnifying the giants of the land and forgetting the miraculous God who delivered them out of Egypt all died in the wilderness.

It is important to realize the witnessing and partaking of miracles from God does not guarantee that someone knows God. About two million Jews were delivered and saw the devastation to the Egyptians, the parting of the Red Sea, the waves crashing down on the Egyptians who pursued them – they saw with their eyes the miracles of God – yet they did not believe. It was more than an error – it was unbelief – no faith – a sin against God. The result was strife or division among the people. Those who cause division God will judge. Joshua and Caleb believed God could surely give them the promised land because He was God who had delivered them out of slavery. They were not focused on the obstacles but on the might of God.

Although you have seen the miracles that God has done for your parents or your friends, it is not enough. You must keep your faith because of God's Word. You must give yourself wholly to God. Even if God has done miracles for you, you cannot trust in the experience as a sign of spiritual maturity. You must continue to press into God especially the Word of God and not allow any weakness, or any success to separate you from God. Don't let poverty or riches separate you from believing God.

Deuteronomy 26: 16 Today the Lord your God has commanded you to do these statutes and judgments. You must therefore keep and do them with all your heart and with all your soul. 17 You have affirmed today that the Lord is your God and vowed to walk in His ways, and to keep His statutes, and His commandments, and His judgments, and to listen to His voice. 18 And the Lord has affirmed today that you are His special people, just as He has promised you, and that you should keep all His commandments. 19 He will exalt you above all nations which He has made, in praise, and in name, and in honor; and that you may be a holy people to the Lord your God, just as He has spoken..

Once you are receiving the favour, prosperity and success promised to God's people who serve Him, worship God and never stop. God often does miracle for His people. Our faith should be in God. Our hope should be in God and our covenant with Him.

God can Open or Shut Doors of Opportunity

By their unbelief, the door that God had opened for them to go into the promised land with victory was closed. God pronounced a judgement that they would wander and could not go in. Some of them reconsidered and spoke that they would go in; they were sorry. It was too late. There are some situations in life where destiny decisions are made and if you do not go the way of faith, you will not get a second chance or you may lose your best chance. The people did not yet revere God as they should and some of them tried to go into the promised land without God and were slain.

Faith is a Requirement

It was not the enemy that was the obstacle to the Israelites obtaining the promised land in that first week; it was their unbelief. God hates unbelief in His people. If we, God's people, do not believe in Him, how can we expect to communicate with Him or receive from Him?

Faith is the main ingredient that God requires from His people. As dollars are our currency in North America, faith is the currency of Heaven.

Hebrews 11: 6 And without faith it is impossible to please God, for he who comes to God must believe that He exists and that He is a rewarder of those who diligently seek Him.

Please realize that Joshua and Caleb could have grown bitter because the people didn't believe them. They too wandered in the wilderness because of the people who sinned against God. Neither of them grew bitter against people or against God; neither of them doubted God or questioned his judgement. They obeyed God and served Moses faithfully until this day at the edge of the Jordan River with Joshua leading.

Joshua the Leader

This same Joshua, who should have inherited his promise because he fully believed God, was standing at the edge of the Jordan River leading the people. God chose Joshua to succeed Moses. God saw Joshua's faith and obedience and chose him as leader to inherit the promises and lead God's people. It was as if those extra forty years of serving with Moses in the wandering of Israel, only caused Joshua and Caleb to grow more in their faith and they grew closer to God. Because they had a faith perspective, they could see the good of each day, learning and believing God. The wilderness did not kill them; it only made their strength stronger.

Joshua believed God. He had seen the potential promise of God forty years previously. He had been willing to go in fighting for the land forty years earlier. He had a good report. He believed God.

As God spoke to Moses to lay hands on Joshua so that he might lead the people into the promised land, God placed the gifts and spiritual anointing on Joshua. The people witnessed this transference of authority. They recognized it was God's choice. They recognized it was with Moses active impartation of anointing (Deuteronomy 31: 7).

Joshua is at the edge of the river, a marker of faith, that he could go over because he believed. He was able to impart to the people his faith and lead them obeying God. The promised land was first promised to Abraham; God remembers His covenants; the land promised to Abraham, Isaac and Jacob/ Israel was there in view, just over the Jordan. God was leading Joshua.

Joshua 1: 6 "Be strong and courageous, for you shall provide the land that I swore to their fathers to give them as an inheritance for this people. 7 Be strong and very courageous, in order to act carefully in accordance with all the law that My servant Moses commanded you. Do not turn aside from it to the right or the left, so that you may succeed wherever you go. 8 This Book of the Law must not depart from your mouth. Meditate on it day and night so that you may act carefully according to all that is written in it. For then you will make your way successful, and you will be wise. 9 Have not I commanded you? Be strong and courageous. Do not be afraid or dismayed, for the Lord your God is with you wherever you go."

I want to examine these words spoken to Joshua.

First, God strengthens him. The word he is commanding to Joshua is for all of Israel as well. They would not all be scattered but they would inherit different parcels of land for each tribe. God designated certain lands for each of the twelve tribes of Israel. Israel was united as a people but each of the tribes had a special place, specially chosen by God. They were given different plots of land to become their own.

God gives Joshua specific instructions to all the Israelites that they should not fear but be strong and courageous. Israel wants to enter the promised land; there is no unbelief as there had been forty years earlier. God tells them to remember the promises that God spoken to Moses. God is reminding them that the promises of God are essential to belief and to pray about, think about and direct their faith towards.

The Torah

God gave the Torah to the people so that they might remember their God. Moses wrote the Torah, the books of Genesis, Exodus, Leviticus, Numbers and Deuteronomy, while in the wilderness. Moses wrote these books imparting the truths that God had taught him and Israel throughout the forty years of wandering and from their birth as a people. He recorded the history of Israel and God's dealings with her. God commands that the Israelites hold on to these words as most precious. These miracles were to be passed on to the next generation. These miracles were to be taught to all children; it was a constant faith builder to Israel – what God had done for them.

God has never changed His Word. The Holy Scriptures are for all of His people. There are special promises made to Israel but we who are Christians are made a joint heir with Jesus Christ upon being born again. We inherit the promises of Abraham through faith, the way Abraham inherited them. The promises made to Moses are for all of us – His people. Jews and Gentiles made one new man through Jesus Christ.

Ephesians 2: 14 For He is our peace, who has made both groups one and has broken down the barrier of the dividing wall, 15 by abolishing in His flesh the enmity, that is, the law of the commandments contained in ordinances, that in Himself He might make the two into one new man, thus making peace, 16 and that He might reconcile both to God into one body through the cross, thereby slaying the enmity.

There is no longer a plan for Jews and a separate plan for Gentiles. We were made one together in Jesus Christ. It is by God's special mercy towards us that we can be partakers of the promises of Abraham by faith. There are special promises to Israel as a nation but all the blessings of the covenant are for all who believe that Jesus is the Messiah.

The Word to Joshua is for you

I am saying the words of Joshua to Israel are for you and I today. God's words of comfort and exhortation or encouragement are for us. If we want to obtain the promises of God, we must press in with faith and with strength. We must believe God's Word. We must obey God. We must keep the promises of God constantly in our hearts, our eyes, our lives. Orthodox Jews literally wear little boxes tied to their hands and their foreheads that contain the promises of God. They are phylacteries. They do it as an outward sign of their honouring these scriptures commanded to Joshua.

I am encouraging you and exhorting you to hold on to the promises of God for you. (Hebrews 10: 23) If you are a Christian, there are promises God has made to you. They are included in the Torah and throughout all the scriptures. The Word of God is God's will for people. God clearly defines what is pleasing to Him and what is not. These words are written so that we would know how to live a life pleasing to God. God promises lists of blessings to His people. If you have never read the book of Deuteronomy, I want to highly recommend it to you. It contains long lists of blessings that will come upon God's faithful people. It also states consequences of disobedience to God.

Promises of God

If you are a new Christian or you do not know the promises of God, use a concordance or Internet sources to research scriptures that have to do with different aspects of life where you need God's blessing. For example, if you are in need of a job, research scriptures such as Deuteronomy 28: 12 or Psalm 90: 17 that speak of God's desire to prosper you in your work.

If you are in need of healing, research scriptures such as Isaiah 53: 5:

But he was wounded for our transgressions,
    he was bruised for our iniquities;
the chastisement of our peace was upon him,
    and by his stripes we are healed.

First, find scriptures that pertain to God's will concerning the thing you are praying about. Get all you can. I write them or print them on index cards, like the kind that would be used to give a speech. I place them together and pray these scriptures regularly. Thank God for them; Believe that God wants you to receive these scriptures as promises. You are a Christian, the promises of God are for you. Read them and reread them; pray them; confess them; pray that God will engraft these words into the core of your being. Keep the Word of God as the highest authority in your life. These are God inspired words that God wants you to know about – that is why we have the Bible. It's not just a history book. The Word of God applies to us today.

Hebrews 4: 12 For the word of God is alive, and active, and sharper than any two-edged sword, piercing even to the division of soul and spirit, of joints and marrow, and able to judge the thoughts and intents of the heart.

God wants us to keep the promises of God as a faith priority. All aspects of human life are covered in the scriptures. God clearly reveals His will in all areas of our lives. It is essential that we read, that we know and that we believe the word of God.

If there are promises of God you are believing for today, that you have not yet received, be encouraged. First of all, believe; God always keeps His promises. Pray that God might help you to see the promises from His point of view. Instead of seeing the obstacles to you achieving or receiving the promises of God, see the promise with faith. Keep that scripture in front of you. Keep them in your sight; read them out loud so your eyes can process the words; listen to them; pray them; believe them; confess them. I mean over and over again until the promises come to pass. Thank God for providing even before you get them. You must be an active participant in receiving your promises. Just as Joshua and Israel had to physically go over Jordan and fight as God instructed them, you and I must obey God.

Do What you can do

Do all you know to do in the natural. If it is getting a job, do all you can do to get the job. Create a good resume; apply to various positions; pray for Divine favour. Connect with people you know might be able to help you. You must do your part. Believe that God can give you favour and give you the job you apply for no matter how many people apply for it because God can make you shine above the others. It's our God who is special – He can place supernatural favour on you so that you obtain the promises of God beyond any earthly obstacle.

Encourage Yourself

Keep encouraging yourself. The best way to do this is to feed your spirit. Sing and praise God with all your being. Keep your relationship with God good. Keep in prayer and praise. Be thankful. Don't let all your relationship with God be about the need. It may be tough but what I am saying is that your relationship with God should be bigger than anything. Continue to worship and praise Him because He is God. Pray for wisdom. There might be some revelation of something you should do or how something should be done. Just as God gave special instruction to Joshua, God may give you special instruction to inherit your promise.

I would recommend you tape your own voice reading the scriptures of promise to you so that you can listen to them. As you hear the word of God, see it with your eyes and pray and confess it with your mouth; you are aligning your life with God's word. That means you believe that God will keep His word to you. As you receive God's Word into your spirit, faith is released. The word of God releases faith as we hear it and receive it. Hearing it isn't the same as hearing and receiving. It isn't the sound of the words themselves but it is your faith mixed with the Word that produces fruit. Faith in God's Word with God's Word produces results.

Hebrews 4: 2 For the gospel was preached to us as well as to them. But the word preached did not benefit them, because it was not mixed with faith in those who heard it.

Build up your Spirit

Be strong in the word of God and your faith in the word of God. Be of good courage – encourage yourself – spiritually. It may include listening to praise and worship music or preaching in addition to the promises. The more you build up your spirit, the stronger you will be and closer to receiving the promises. Get into church services that teach the Word of God with faith believing it applies to our lives today. Supplement your regular church preaching with Internet preaching and teaching, books, CD's or DVD's that preach and teach faith. We are so privileged in North America to get so much of God's word to encourage us on TV or radio or Internet etc. Thank God for freedom of worship!

Be Careful What you put into Yourself

Don't fill your eyes or ears with unbelief. Do not listen to things that are negative, You may have to throw out some of your cd's. Do not give yourself to any type of game or entertainment that compromises God's word – that means sins against God and His Word. If you are serious about God, those things should be repulsive to you. Pray that you would love what God loves and hate what He hates. This might mean you pray for God to watch over you, giving you discernment that you would not be partaking of unbelief or fear through media. The Holy Spirit can prompt you when to turn things off or turn away from things that will try to contaminate your faith.

Just as Satan as the serpent in Genesis enticed and tempted Eve and Adam, he will try to get you from believing in God`s words the same way.

Genesis 3: 4 Then the serpent said to the woman, "You surely will not die! 5 For God knows that on the day you eat of it your eyes will be opened and you will be like God, knowing good and evil."

He twisted God`s words and caused doubt and unbelief to enter in Eve and Adam so they saw the fruit on the tree; it appealed to them sensually; it was desirable – they believed the evil words of the serpent rather than the words of God who told them not to eat of it.

God promised the Holy Scriptures. Jesus didn`t throw out the Old Testament – all the teachings. He fulfilled the scriptures and sealed them as a covenant to us through his blood shed on Calvary. Jesus died for our salvation, our healing, our deliverance, our prosperity. All the effects of the curse that were placed on Adam and Eve because of their disobedience – their sin against God – Jesus died to pay the penalty so that we could truly receive the blessings promised to Abraham, Isaac, Jacob etc. Jesus died so that we who are not Israelis by birth could be born from above, born again could be grafted into Him.

We who are Gentiles by birth could never have the promises before in the same way. Jesus` side was pierced on Calvary. This was an act of proving he had died to the Romans and Jews. It was also a place where symbolically, we could be grafted in as believers in God. It is this same place where Jews who do not know Jesus can be grafted in once more as was spoken by Paul.

Romans 11: 17 But if some of the branches were broken off, and you, being a wild olive shoot, were grafted in among them and became a partaker with them of the root and richness of the olive tree, 18 do not boast against the branches. If you boast, remember you do not sustain the root, but the root sustains you. 19 You will say then, "The branches were broken off, so that I might be grafted in." 20 This is correct. They were broken off because of unbelief, but you stand by faith. Do not be arrogant, but fear. 21 For if God did not spare the natural branches, neither will He spare you.

By Faith We Receive

Jesus blood shed for us cleanses us but also seals us as a people of covenant with God. Jesus gives us the fullness of the blessings of the covenant God had with Israel. By faith in the Blood of Jesus as the sacrifice necessary to redeem us to God, we receive by faith in Jesus Christ alone our inheritance in Christ. It is not by any works but by faith alone in Jesus and His blood.

Romans 8: 17 and if children, then heirs: heirs of God and joint-heirs with Christ, if indeed we suffer with Him, that we may also be glorified with Him.

By Jesus resurrection, the blessings of Abraham and all the covenants of the Old Testament are fulfilled. We who believe on Jesus Christ are made joint heirs with Jesus of all of the promises of God. That should make you want to dance. Faith in Jesus means covenant with Jesus – total relationship with God. Part of the blessing was sent on the Day of Pentecost – the baptism of the Holy Spirit. God gave us His Spirit so that we might be filled with His indwelling presence. We are strengthened and empowered by the Holy Spirit who lives in us.

The Baptism of the Holy Spirit

The Baptism of the Holy Spirit is for all Christians. If you are not yet baptized in the Holy Spirit, the good news is that you can be. The Baptism of the Holy Spirit gives you power to witness for Christ. There are gifts and blessings because of it; it is a language that is spiritual that makes it possible for you to commune with God in a special way. By praying in tongues, an evidence of the Baptism of the Holy Spirit, we can stir up other Spiritual Gifts and God can use us or speak to us. God lives on the inside of us and prays for us. That is exciting. It is not about making a way to God – He made the way to raise us up. Jesus is the way – the only way. His Spirit in us gives us boldness to do the works of Christ on the earth,

Acts 2: 38 Peter said to them, "Repent and be baptized, every one of you, in the name of Jesus Christ for the forgiveness of sins, and you shall receive the gift of the Holy Spirit. 39 For the promise is to you, and to your children, and to all who are far away, as many as the Lord our God will call."

Hold on to the Promises of God

If you have some promises you are believing God for, hold on to those promises in faith. Fill your ears and your eyes with faith preaching. Read the promises. Pray them for yourself. Thank God for them. Don't share them with just anyone. They are precious to you, only share them with people who believe the same as you and you believe will pray in agreement with you. Only share it with people of like precious faith – they are people who love you and want God's will for you. They care for you and would pray as if it were for themselves – only God's best for you.

There are people who you know that you agree with. They are usually your closest friends, or family – Christians who believe the same that you would want to influence your kids and your family. They add value. They give you the best; they are people of excellence who give God the best. They are Christians in public or in private. They are the kind of people as Joshua and Caleb or Daniel who lived their faith and are known thousands of years later because of their true witness – living their lives wholly for God's glory.

Even Joshua and Caleb, after they had wandered in the wilderness with the unbelievers, kept their faith. Joshua and Caleb were stronger after those years; their faith was sharpened. Even in their 80's, they with boldness said "Give me this mountain". They knew God had promised them that land 40 years previously and they wanted it. They were strong and willing to fight to get what God promised them.

It because they believed God's promise more than anything. Do you want what God has promised you? Even if it has been years and it has not yet come. Do you want what God has promised? Stir up your faith for it. Say it out loud so your ears can hear – "Yes. I want the promises of God. Yes. I want what God promised me. I believe He will give it to me as He promised. I receive by faith what God has promised."

Choose to believe God. If He promised you something and it hasn't happened yet, pray asking God for what you can do. If there was any area of disobedience to something He instructed to you, repent and obey whatever He commanded you to do. If there is no known disobedience, pray asking God for wisdom for what you should do. Sometimes God promises something and there is an immediate release of it in your life. Sometimes, God promises something and it does not come for a while.

Please know if those promises involve other people, God will never force someone to do His will. God will bring all things into alignment with His will – but He fill not force His will. He gives people opportunities to be part of His plan. Sometimes part of the waiting for the promise is God wooing people to be participants in His will.

Waiting in Faith

It doesn't mean we just remain passive and wait. No. Wait in faith, praying, doing God's will in all areas where you know what to do, do it. Be faithful. Be diligent to do all of what you know to do. Your faithfulness in all areas of your life align you in the proper position to receive the promises. Keep building up yourself in the faith. Keep doing good works such as giving, serving, living Holy. Keep the promises fresh through prayer and thanksgiving. Pray for others.

Sometimes, God may tug at your heart connected to a ministry or project going on that seemingly has nothing to do with your life. Sometimes, God will move on your heart to give financially and prayerfully to that ministry. Do it in obedience to God. Wrap your faith around your giving believing that God will honour your gift and release angels to bring the word of God to you to come to pass. You yourself pray and ask God to release angels to perform it. This is an area I must emphasize because angels align things in the unseen realm just as your faithfulness aligns things in the natural and spiritual realms.

Sow scripture into your own life. Listen to Spirit filled worship and praise music. Listen to preaching that builds up your spirit. There have been seasons where I played and played prophetic preaching over and over day after day for months while I was believing and expecting God to keep His word to me. Follow the prompting of the Holy Spirit. In these seasons of expectation and faith building, eliminate anything that does not build your faith. If it does not add to your faith, cut it out of your life. It may be temporary or it may be permanent.

I am talking about radical faith. Even things that are good and not sinful, if they do not add to your faith, should be omitted from your life. Sports, entertainment, leisure activities, all of them wholesome, good activities, might need to be eliminated from your life temporarily. I give an example here of radical faith. It is not for everyday life; it is for a critical situation. If you are serious about obtaining your answer to prayer, your promise from God, your miracle, be sensitive to the Holy Spirit. You may be prompted to read your Bible instead of eat lunch with your friends. You might feel a prompting to not play volleyball or a hockey for a season. It might only be temporary. There have been instances in my life where this has happened to me because I knew I had to focus on God to align properly so that my miracle or a miracle for others I was praying for would occur.

Fasting

There are different types of fasting. They are not ways to leverage God into giving you something. Fasting is self-denial for the purpose of seeking God. It is a way to show you are serious about God and that it is more important to you than daily food. There are many types of fasts.

Without Food

One type of fast is the Jesus fast. That is doing without food or water for a period. Please notice, going without water for longer than 3 or 3 days is rare and should not be done if you have health issues etc. All sorts of cautions go up when I offer this as a choice. Usually 2 or 3 days is the maximum for this type of self-denial. What you do is focus on God instead of your food or drink. Matthew 4: 2 describes Jesus in the wilderness fasting.

Daniel Fast

Daniel 1: 13 Then let our countenances be looked upon before you, and the countenance of the youths who eat of the portion of the king's food. And as you see, deal with your servants." 14 So he consented to them in this matter and tested them for ten days.

Daniel and His friends would not defile themselves with bloody meat sacrificed to idols. They would not drink the wine dedicated to a pagan god. They ate fruit and vegetables only and drank water. Many people choose this method of fasting because it is easier than a total fast from all food. It doesn't mean it isn't effective. Its effectiveness has to do with your faith and the reason you are fasting.

Liquid Fast

During this period, the person drinks but does not eat. It is effective because it gives you some nourishment but you know you are going without food to devote yourself to prayer and faith. Fruit juice, beverages, can give you nutrients. There are health benefits to this type of fasting but the person who uses it is doing it to get closer to God.

Partial Fast

The person may give up desserts or meat or something he or she enjoys such as TV or Internet etc. This is a way of showing God you are serious.

Please note there are all types of fasting. Fasting and prayer has a mighty effect on aligning you in position with God for a miracle.

The important thing is obeying the prompting of the Holy Spirit within you. If you are not sure which fast to do, pray and ask the Holy Spirit to lead you.

During these seasons of fasting, only watch things that add to your faith. Only listen to things that add to your faith. If it does not build your faith, keep away from those things until the end of the season. Go the way of spirit during these periods. Choose the way that directly builds up and encourages you. Choose the way of living in the Holy Spirit and being led by the Spirit. It may mean you pray more, praise more, focus on God more. If you are single, you are free to do this. A married person should speak with his or her spouse and get agreement to do it. It is not something you boast about or announce publicly. It is something between you and God a Holy consecration for a duration.

Matthew 6: 16 "Moreover, when you fast, do not be like the hypocrites with a sad countenance. For they disfigure their faces so they may appear to men to be fasting. Truly I say to you, they have their reward. 17 But you, when you fast, anoint your head and wash your face, 18 so that you will not appear to men to be fasting, but to your Father who is in secret. And your Father who sees in secret will reward you openly.

Philippians 4: 8 Finally, brothers, whatever things are true, whatever things are honest, whatever things are just, whatever things are pure, whatever things are lovely, whatever things are of good report, if there is any virtue, and if there is any praise, think on these things. 9 Do those things which you have both learned and received, and heard and seen in me, and the God of peace will be with you.

During these special periods or expecting and believing for a promise, a miracle or answer to prayer, do not associate with just anyone. You can, but it isn't in your best interest. Only get with people of the same faith and who love you and care about your spirit. If they do not care for you as if for their own selves, cut them out of your life during that period.

Joshua and Caleb shared the vision of what God promised them. They were close. They were both believing and living lives of excellence and were living proof that God gave them the promised land. They entered their promise because of it. Use discernment, pray for it and ask God to show you who those people of like precious faith are.

You cannot yoke an ox and a donkey together. Both animals were used by farmers to help do work on the farm. But an ox walks with a particular gate and a donkey in a different way. A yoke was a device made of wood or metal used so a team of oxen or animals could be used. Today we use tractors. You cannot be equally unyoked; unbelievers or even people of faith who are not in your faith zone at present, cannot be a part of your life for that season or you will notice things are not going smoothly – both of you in different directions. I am talking about people who you share your dreams with, people who you let pray for you or for your kids, people who are closest to you. It is not some weird super spiritual thing. Those in your closest circle must be like- minded or they can't be there.

Christian Media

There have been periods of my own life, because I was the first Christian in my family, that I connected with ministries from TV and the Internet. I sowed financially and prayerfully and sent my prayer requests to them because I needed an answer to prayer; I wanted and needed a miracle; I had no close who I could pray in agreement with me. I thank God for Christian media and the difference it's made to my life. Truly some of those ministries made an impact on my life as certain points in my life that a miracle is what was required.

Thanksgiving

If God has given you the promise or you are on the edge of receiving a promise from God and it was something significant, be thankful. Thank God in songs of praise and thanksgiving that you offer to Him privately. Let the Holy Spirit lead you so that you can praise and worship God with the new song of the LORD, specific praise for a special answer to prayer. Praise God publicly. Tell people what God has done for you. You may want to celebrate by buying gifts for people. You may want to host a party of celebration. Most certainly give God glory for what He has done for you and don't forget it. Always remember what God did for you. Listen, I've received some promises from God. Don't act as if it is nothing. Thank God – not just once but constantly remember His faithfulness.

Giving

There was a period in my life I was praying for a job and praying, but years passed. I believed God wanted me to have a job. I remember a preacher on TV preaching a message about giving a substantial gift of money and believing God for a promised. It was a sowing of finances (or goods) believing God would supply for you. It was a type of radical giving – like fasting so that you would be aligned in position to receive from God. I did not have a substantial gift of money that I could give. The preacher's words were not surface. I knew God was speaking to me through that preacher. I said within myself " I will give it as soon as I get a job." I sowed an amount that I could give. Once more money came, I sowed again for this purpose.

It didn't come immediately but it came, an answer to prayer. It was exactly what I wanted. God gave me the desire of my heart. I was so excited seeing the faithfulness of God to me, I couldn't contain myself. I thanked God. I thank God even know for it. As soon as I could I gave a significant amount of money into a ministry that had helped me. I felt so strongly about it that I did it yearly. I began giving to God above what I had ever done in the past. It was a release of giving to show gratitude. I didn't have to do it. I did it because it is what I wanted. It is what I felt strongly to do. I began to take a second job so I could give more. I knew that my giving was going to the gospel. Giving is an expression of worship. Just as I praise and worship God, I gave money, substantial amounts (for me) not wanting something, but because I want to thank God.

If God has done something for you, never forget it. Remain in a thankful position. Thank Him. Give your testimony of how God answered your prayer and gave you your promise. Always give honour to God for what He has given you. Remain in a posture of thanksgiving. Thank God so that all the people in your life can see what God done for you. Also, the angels can witness what God has done for you. It matters in all realms of your authority. Your thanksgiving releases faith into others and gives glory to God.

Deuteronomy 26: 10 Now, indeed, I have brought the first fruits of the land, which you, O Lord, have given me." Then you must set it before the Lord your God and worship before the Lord your God. 11 You must rejoice in every good thing which the Lord your God has given to you and your house, you, and the Levite, as well as the foreigner who is among you.

Keep the Word – Be an Overcomer

Romans 8: 31 What then shall we say to these things? If God is for us, who can be against us? 32 He who did not spare His own Son, but delivered Him up for us all, how shall He not with Him also freely give us all things?

Vs 37 No, in all these things we are more than conquerors through Him who loved us. 38 For I am persuaded that neither death nor life, neither angels nor principalities nor powers, neither things present nor things to come, 39 neither height nor depth, nor any other created thing, shall be able to separate us from the love of God, which is in Christ Jesus our Lord.

The Apostle Paul

The Apostle Paul suffered much in his life because he had become a Christian. It was a miraculous conversion and he could not deny Christ. He was stoned, beaten and eventually martyred because of his faith. His life was radically changed after he became a Christian.

He had been a Pharisee, a teacher of God's laws. He was esteemed highly by those around him. He had also been against Christianity until Jesus appeared to him on the road to Damascus. In the exact same places he had Christians arrested and killed, he started preaching that Jesus was the Christ. The Pharisees turned against him and would have killed him if he was not helped to escape.

Despite these things, Paul is writing to the Church in Romans stating that God was with him. His encounter with Christ was so mighty that it influenced his destiny. He gave up all that he had for Christ and to preach Christ.

Turning Towards God

If you have truly received Jesus Christ as your Saviour and LORD, you will not hide it. You will not want to hide it. Your life will be transformed and you will want to share the good news of Salvation through Jesus Christ with as many people as you can. You will begin to love Christians and want to be with them. You will be strengthened in corporate worship and praise. You will no longer want to do sinful things or things that in any way go against Christ. Once you have accepted Jesus Christ, you have been set free from sin and the consequences of sin. You are in the kingdom of light. You realize that you are free. You realize that you can do anything you want. In your heart, there will be a passionate desire for God. You will want to press in to know God. You will realize that turning towards God means you turn away from some things.

Turning towards God means you may leave old associations and join with a new group of people. It means you will begin to hate evil and begin to love truth. You will want to live your life pleasing to God. You will want to press in to know more of God realizing He is a living God living on the inside of you. You will realize that as you pray, God speaks to you. You will realize the Word of God is your treasure. In the Word of God is comfort, peace, life.

Your life becomes transformed. Your character is changed. I cannot describe the change in terms of nature because no other occurrence is like it – the new birth is the start of new life – learning who you are as a new creation in Christ. You will begin to display the fruit of the Spirit. You will begin to become more like the God you know. Compassion, love, giving, mercy, gentleness, temperance, kindness, peace, joy, humility and meekness will become your character traits as the Holy Spirit transforms you Galatians 5: 22 "But the fruit of the Spirit is love, joy, peace, patience, gentleness, goodness, faith, 23 meekness, and self-control; against such there is no law." You will desire to be more like God. You will want to live Holy because you have encountered the Holy God and recognize what it is to be without sin because of Jesus' blood shed for you.

The View

You will no longer view things the same. With Jesus Christ's Holy Spirit living in you, you will begin to see potential and possibilities, your priorities will change as you desire spiritual food of the Word of God. Your outlook will change; you will begin to think of things in light of eternity.

I want to compare before you accepted Christ as seeing through a glass, but seeing life after you were born again serving the LORD Jesus Christ as though it were from a prism, the rainbows of colours showing their manifold beauty and potential as the light shines through it. You can see the beauty of the rainbow colours as the light catches ion the crystal glass. You will become fascinated by it. You will become fascinated with Jesus Christ and the things of God. You will want to know Him and will enjoy being in His presence.

Knowing

You know if you have encountered Christ. Some people experience feeling – such as goose bumps or literal shaking of the body trembling in God's holiness. Some people are overwhelmed by joy and gladness and may even begin laughing. Others may weep and weep because they know God paid the price for our eternal life. Usually when you first encounter Christ there is weeping, because you realize the cost of your salvation and that there was no way you could have ever been worthy. You realize the sacrifice of Jesus makes you Holy. It is the mercy of God that lets us know our need for a Saviour. We know by the Spirit and begin to have our spiritual discernment developed.

Isaiah 53: 5 But he was wounded for our transgressions,
 he was bruised for our iniquities;
the chastisement of our peace was upon him,
 and by his stripes we are healed

As a born again, Spirit filled Christian, you know that God is for you. You know because He lives in you and you live in Him. There is confidence because of your relationship with God. No matter what you may be facing, you can and should always encourage yourself because you know God saved you. God's mercy towards you let you learn about Him. Remember the miracle that God did for you in in Salvation. That's the same God with you today.

Remember Your Salvation

You must remember what God did for you regularly. Usually, we do it at the Lord's supper or communion, but that is not nearly enough. The fact that God drew you to Himself and placed people in your life to witness to you and give you understanding so that you would come to know Him should be always a rejoicing as you realize God made a way to reach you even though you may have been going the direct opposite direction. God sent people you needed to lead you so that you could repent and turn to Christ. As I remember my own salvation and the events of my life surrounding it, I rejoice with thanksgiving and wonder. I know that I know God orchestrated things on earth and in the heavens to reach me. I know that I know God delivered me. Oh, as you think of your own salvation – meditate on it and know that God who saved you is the God who can keep you.

Remember What God has Done For You

Remember the day you got saved as though it were your birthday. Keep it in your heart as special. Also, get yourself to remember the answers to prayer He has given you. Make a list of what God has done for you. If He has healed you, thank Him for it. If He delivered you from addictions, praise Him for it; if He Baptized you in the Holy Spirit, thank God for it. Remembering what God has done for you is a sure way to encourage yourself in the LORD.

Jude 1: 20 But you, beloved, build yourselves up in your most holy faith. Pray in the Holy Spirit. 21 Keep yourselves in the love of God while you are waiting for the mercy of our Lord Jesus Christ, which leads to eternal life.

1 Samuel 30: 6b But David encouraged himself in the Lord his God.

Be an Encourager

Share what God has done for you with others. Make a list of things God has done for you since you have been saved. Share those things with your family members so they know God has answered prayer for you. Write those things. They are your testimonies of God`s faithfulness to you. By speaking those things to others, your own faith is also stirred.

Live in Your Spirit.

If you are going through a rough situation, encourage yourself in the LORD. It is awesome that sometimes God sends angels to encourage people like Daniel (Daniel 9). It is awesome that sometimes God send messengers or people to encourage you (Paul was refreshed by his spiritual children such as Timothy). Sometimes though, you have got to refresh your own self in the LORD. That means feeding yourself things that will encourage, edify, exhort, comfort and build yourself up. You should start in what He has done for you and how good he has been to you but you don't have to stop there. Begin to praise Him for the answers to prayer you haven't yet seen. Begin to thank God for miraculously providing a way for you. As you begin to praise God in this way, you will be releasing joy and faith.

You and I do not often see the real enemy. It isn't people. There is a spirit world of angels and demons that engage in warfare over our lives. The scriptures instruct us to put on the armour of God. Most of the armour is to defend us.

Ephesians 6: 11 Put on the whole armor of God that you may be able to stand against the schemes of the devil. 12 For our fight is not against flesh and blood, but against principalities, against powers, against the rulers of the darkness of this world, and against spiritual forces of evil in the heavenly places

Armor of God

Ephesians 6: 13 Therefore take up the whole armor of God that you may be able to resist in the evil day, and having done all, to stand. 14 Stand therefore, having your waist girded with truth, having put on the breastplate of righteousness, 15 having your feet fitted with the readiness of the gospel of peace, 16 and above all, taking the shield of faith, with which you will be able to extinguish all the fiery arrows of the evil one. 17 Take the helmet of salvation and the sword of the Spirit, which is the word of God.

I believe it is more than an analogy that the apostle is giving us in this scripture. I literally pray the armour of God on as I would put on clothing each day. As you pray it on that God that He covers all those parts of your body, soul and spirit.

Helmet of salvation – The joy of your salvation is your strength.

Breastplate of righteousness – Just as the physical armour covered the delicate areas – pray that God will keep your heart pure and upright.

Girdle of truth – Pray that truth will be covering you as a belt. Most tool belts are made to carry what you must have. Truth is a strong and mighty force or righteousness. Jesus is truth. Jesus bore witness on the earth as truth. Keep the testimony that knowing Jesus is truth.

Shoes of Peace – Isaiah 52: 7 Blessed are the feet that bring the good news of the gospel. Pray that each place you go you will be bringing the gospel of peace. Acknowledge that Jesus is the prince of Peace.

Shield of faith – The shield is a main defence against weapons. You can stir up yourself by remembering what God has done for you. You can also read the scriptures and pray read the scriptures as prayers for what God will yet do for you. The Word of God releases faith as we say it, hear it, confess it, pray it and live it. The Word of God releases faith. Faith is a shield that covers you and repels weapons.

Sword of the Word of God – The Word of God is not only a protection or encouragement to you but it is a weapon. Read scriptures that the Holy Spirit has spoken or quickened to you. As you pray these scriptures and confess them, they fight against the enemy of your soul. Speaking and confessing God's Word releases angels to bring the Word to come to pass concerning you. It is ammunition against the enemy and it is protection for you.

The Word of God

The Word of God is vital for your spiritual life. The Word of God is beautiful and it is powerful. It is our spiritual food because it strengthens us. It is our spiritual strength because it gives us knowledge and understanding of spiritual things. It is a shield to us. It is a sword to us. It releases the fruit of the spirit as we pray it and believe it. The Word of God was written by holy men inspired by God. These people obeyed God and we have the Holy Scriptures as a record of God's will for us. The Word of God covers all major aspects of human life. There are scriptures pertaining to all the main things a person may need in life.

It brings spiritual nourishment to us when it is mixed with faith – it produces godly character and miraculous transformational strength. Simultaneously as we learn God's Word, it becomes a weapon to defeat any enemy. God's Word is settled. It is established. It is unchangeable.

Psalm 119:
89 Forever, O Lord, Your word
   is established in heaven.

Psalm 138: 2 I will worship toward Your holy temple,
   and praise Your name
   for Your lovingkindness and for Your truth;
for You have exalted Your word
   above all Your name.

The Name of Jesus

Jesus name is the highest name where by people may be saved. Jesus name is a weapon to those who know Him. He covers us with His blood and should an enemy approach us, we plead the blood of Jesus. That means we literally pray that Jesus blood protects us. Jesus is the only name that can bring salvation. Jesus is the only one who gave his life for you.

The Word of God

The Word of God is even above the name of God. This is too hard to describe. The two are inseparable – God enforces His Word with His name but the Word of God, the Holy Scriptures give us information on the past, on the present and the future.

People – God can put the right people in your life at the exact moment you need them. Often these are referred to as Divine Connections. These are intersections where one or more people come into your life and the result is that your grow, are strengthened, built up and established because of them.

It usually starts before we know it with people praying for us before we are saved. Someone will start feeling a desire to pray for our salvation. Afterwards, it includes those who will teach us things such as the foundations of our faith, main doctrines of Christ and how to live a godly Holy life. This usually leads us to a local church where we are spiritually nourished and become contributing members to the body of Christ there.

Christians require other Christians to pray with, to worship with and to build up and encourage; we use our spiritual gifts this way. We use our discernment. We learn to love each other because of our close fellowship or friendship with other Christians.

As we pray with other Christians, our faith is not only built up but it is multiplied because Jesus is there in a different way than if we pray alone. There is a spiritual dynamic that happens when Christians gather together. It is though the kingdom of God shines brightly during the gathering.

Matthew 18: 19 "Again I say to you, that if two of you agree on earth about anything they ask, it will be done for them by My Father who is in heaven. 20 For where two or three are assembled in My name, there I am in their midst."

Most often if you are in a rough spot of life, a Christian will encourage you with a scripture or a song or a kind word. We, the body of Christ are made to build up encourage and strengthen each other. God can send an angel to speak to you and He does this sometimes. There are testimonies of angels appearing to people or Jesus Christ Himself appearing to people, but most often, God uses people. God can use the words of your own mouth to encourage you and strengthen you.

Because words come from the heart, if you have words that are faith filled testimonies of what has done for you, you can be built up in faith by releasing those words.

Your testimony is a weapon.

Revelation 12 : 11 They overcame him
  by the blood of the Lamb
  and by the word of their testimony,
and they loved not their lives
  unto the death.

The Blood of the Lamb – only Jesus blood could ever save you, Your own righteousness is as filthy rags (Is 64: 6) . Literally asking Jesus to cover you by His blood repels the enemy or demons because they know they cannot resist the power of Jesus victory over death and hell and the grave. They know Jesus is Messiah. His blood defeated them.

The word of your testimony – we should not only stir our faith in rough spots. We should be doing it daily. We should always have a Word of encouragement to share with people causing them to know the reason for our hope in Christ. Sharing what Christ has done for you not only encourages someone, it encourages you. You should be sharing with people how you came to Christ. You should be sharing with people, the answers to prayer you have received and how Christ has transformed your life.
1 Peter 3: 15 But sanctify the Lord God in your hearts. Always be ready to give an answer to every man who asks you for a reason for the hope that is in you, with gentleness and fear.

God Answers Prayer

Whether you are a new Christian or a seasoned Christian, you know that you know God has answered your prayers. God provides for you; God lets you know in the most inner self that He has answered your prayers. This ought to be part of our testimony. God did such and such in answer to prayer.

Loving not your Life – This doesn't mean you hate life. It is just the opposite. You realize the gift God gave you in your life and you desire to give Him the best of your life each day. Literally, you present yourself to God daily: spirit, soul and body.

Romans 12: 1 I urge you therefore, brothers, by the mercies of God, that you present your bodies as a living sacrifice, holy, and acceptable to God, which is your reasonable service of worship. 2 Do not be conformed to this world, but be transformed by the renewing of your mind, that you may prove what is the good and acceptable and perfect will of God.

A Christian who values his or her life will want to give the best to God because he or she knows God has always given His best. It would mean making a commitment to pray, to serve, to give etc. It means all your priorities change once you are sold out to God. You choose to wholly give yourself to God. The more you know Christ, the more you love Him. You want to be more like Him. As you press in to God, never stop. All of eternity you can spend learning about God. You can press in and throughout all eternity God can be revealing His glory to you and giving you wisdom, knowledge, joy, etc.

More than a Conqueror

Yes. Oh yes. You can know that you are more than a conqueror. Jesus Christ triumphed over death but also over sin and hell. Jesus gave us authority over all of the earth with a commandment to preach the gospel all over the earth (Luke 10:19). All authority means, Jesus will use us to be His ministers in the earth. It includes healing the sick, casting out demons, and preaching good news to people who don't know about Jesus and encouraging each other – literally doing the works of Christ on the earth. That means as we speak in faith, or preach in faith, God releases angels to go perform the things we are preaching about or ministering. It means that Jesus through the Holy Spirit living inside of you will lay hands on the sick and they will recover.

You will not know you are more than a conqueror if you don't believe Jesus' words. You must confess the words over yourself. It is Jesus who is the Saviour, the Healer and the Deliverer but He uses us. Our willingness to be used and our obedience are keys to victory in ministry or in our personal lives. Christ has done all He is going to do. He gave us the victory but we must believe it and act upon it in faith. Faith is the substance that quickens the word of God so that you can minister, so that you can live victoriously, so that you can be confident in all areas of your life.

It is God's will for you to prosper. It is God's will for you to be healthy. It is God's will for you to live in freedom with joy. God clearly tells us these things throughout the Bible – especially in the book of

Deuteronomy (Deut. 28) God fights for us. He will send angels to rescue us (Psalm 34:7). He will lead us faithfully by the Holy Spirit. Normal Christian living is living in the realm of the supernatural.

That doesn't mean we don't have an enemy. The devil would do whatever he can to stop Christians. I thank God, I live in a democracy. We have freedom of worship in North America and most of the Western world. We must live our lives faithfully obeying God's Word and not giving into flesh or sin. We lay down our freedom to sin because living for Jesus brings life, health, strength, peace, joy. Live in holiness to be pleasing to God. Sin always ends in death. Sin, always separates us from God. It is important to remember that not all Christians have the same freedoms we do.

A Christian who is martyred is victorious. Please realize it is not for most of us to be martyred, but in some places on earth (too many to mention) there is persecution of Christians; they are forced to deny Christ or die. Should you be in such a position, pray that God will strengthen you until the end of your life. Even though you may die – you win. You will be in the eternal presence of Jesus. Christian martyrs lives are not in vain. They demonstrated the love of God in the earth while they lived; they kept their faith until the end, they will receive a victor's crown from Jesus Himself (Revelation 2: 10).

Boldness About Christ Living in us

We Christians should be have boldness about our faith. The fact that God lives on the inside of us makes us special. We should want others to experience the blessings of knowing God as we have. Part of the testimony is sharing that Jesus Christ actually lives on the inside of us. It is Christ living in us that is our hope, that is our glory. Christ alone in us and through us, gets all the glory.

Jesus is with us in the day to day normal life activities, but He is also with us during the high points of life or if tragedy comes. God will never leave us. His constant abiding presence is our joy. Christ can shine through us by our kind words, kind acts, goodness, gentleness, mercy, serving etc. Christians will love people because God loves people. We will care and our unique expression of Christ's love for others is like a light that shines brightly. God's character shines like a diamond reflecting light to all of those around you.

You are more than a conqueror – you need to speak it over your own self. Say what God's Word says about you. Don't believe anything above the priority of God's Word. God's Word is always true. Come into agreement with it. It involves faith. Faith comes by hearing the word. Begin confessing it, praying it, singing it. God's Word brings faith. It reminds you – as you speak it and hear it with your own ears, that God is for you. As you confess it, the angelic realm also hears it. Angels begin to use the word to defend you and protect you and release blessings towards you. Demons begin to tremble and will have to leave you alone. They cannot stay in an atmosphere of faith.

Keep encouraging yourself. Jesus Christ has overcome all things and you are joint heir with Jesus Christ.

1.   Confess the word that you are more than a conqueror.
2.   Remind yourself of the victories God has given to you in the past. If God has set you free – remind yourself of it. Tell others they can be set free. God gets all the glory and you release faith into people's lives and in your own self.
3.   It is always excellent to remind yourself of the blood of Jesus. Remember it in communion, yes. Remember it on special occasions. If things are rough, start talking about the blood of Jesus. Start singing about the blood of Jesus. Nothing of the enemy can stay as you talk about or sing about the blood of the lamb.
4.   Encourage the Christians in your life. Tell them what God has done for you. God can use your answers to pray to release faith in others. If God doesn't give you a scripture to speak to a brother or scripture, tell him or her what God has done for you. Leave a deposit of Christ in the people you encounter. Share something that would encourage, build up, strengthen them. They will know by the spirit of God that you are speaking life to them. Yes- two Christians together should be as iron sharpening iron (Proverbs 27: 17). Our words should encourage each other.

3 SOWING TO THE SPIRIT

Sow to the Spirit that you might reap of the Spirit. Usually, at the start of a new year, we emphasize self-improvement resolutions. If you are reading this and it is the start of a new year – certainly apply it, but even if it is not the start of a new calendar year but it is a place of new consecration to God – please consider these words. This chapter is on how to sow into yourself that you might strengthen, build up, establish yourself in the faith.

Sometimes a word is spoken by your pastor or some other preacher. Sometimes, you yourself are reading the Word of God and a scripture jumps out at you and you know God is drawing you closer. These are fresh opportunities to give yourself wholly to God. As you do it, God is always so merciful to us that His Spirit comforts us, teaches us and directs us.

Sowing

First, there must be sowing of prayer. This involves praising, worshipping, talking to God, praying for ourselves, pressing in to know what the Holy Spirit has to say to us. It isn't that God isn't willing to talk to us; often we don't press in to listen to what God has to say. It involves listening to the leading of the Holy Spirit. Pray, thanking God, praising Him but also make your petitions know to Him. That means, ask Him for what you have need of. It means praying for your spirit, soul and body. It means claiming the blessings of Deuteronomy that God gave to Israel as His covenant people. We accept Jesus' sacrifice for our lives making us inheritors of the New Covenant in Christ Jesus. The blessings are for us because of Jesus.

It means praying for others. It is something we can do because we are Christians. God speaks in different ways to us. For example, the most usual way is for God to quicken the scriptures to us. God speaks through His Word. Also, God uses pastors and teachers to speak to us and quicken scriptures to us or things we ought to consider. God can use friends or associates or strangers. God can impress upon our spiritual inner man that we aught do something. It usually seems so ordinary that we may not be sure it is God. For instance, a thought may come such as pray for so and so. It could be a family member or friend or someone we don't really know but know of. What I mean by this is that God can involve us in ministry by inspiring us to pray for others.

There are so many testimonies of people who have received impressions and obeyed and prayed for the person and later found out at that exact moment someone's life was saved from a disaster or collision but was saved from it by some weird instance. I have obeyed these promptings myself driving. I would feel a strong prompting to drive a different route than usual and by doing it was a slight inconvenience or seemingly unimportant thing until later I saw there may have been a collision, or a train or some other hindrance that I missed by following the prompting.

God may nudge you politely such as what I have explained. God may give you a dream or a vision that directs you. God may send an angel to minister to you. There are so many ways God can speak to us; there is no limit. The most normal way is through scripture or a nudge in your spirit. We have been given the awesome privilege of being a co labourer with Christ. God will use us to pray for people so angels can be released to bring answers or miracles build is an effective way to build up yourself in the Spirit. The Apostle Paul stated that he prayed in tongues more than anyone (1 Corinthians 14:18). I don't believe he was doing this to brag but to show the importance of tongues in the life of a Christian. Romans 8: 26 explains to us that as we pray in the spirit we are praying with groanings that cannot be uttered.

What happens is the Holy Spirit gives us words to pray and as we pray them out loud, we are praying God's perfect will for people or situations, even though we may not know what we are praying. Sometimes, God gives us the interpretation of what we are praying. Sometimes, we pray in tongues, pray in English back and forth. Often during praying in tongues, the Holy Spirit quickens things to me in my spirit and I say them out loud such as "Yes I will go there." Or some other thing that seems random – but it was really what the Holy Spirit was praying through you bringing it as a priority to your life.

Pray in Tongues Strong and Long

I am saying pray in tongues for your own self on purpose. Yes pray for others in tongues; yes pray for other things in tongues but I am especially encouraging you to pray in tongues for your own self. You may wonder why and you may wonder how long. I have explained why – because you are praying with your spirit things that only the Holy Spirit knows about and knows how to pray about. How long is something only you and God can determine but I can tell you if you are asking that question, you are not praying in tongues long enough.

Years ago, I heard Kenneth Hagin Sr. preaching on praying in tongues and he gave us a challenge. He said that if we wanted a radical change, a miracle to try it. It was to pray in tongues every day for 1 hour. He said if the situation hadn't radically changed within 30 days to write him. I started doing it. At first it was tough like paddling up stream. It did not come easily because I wasn't used to it. After a while, I started praying and praising and God was quickening me in the gifts of the Spirit so strong that I started being used by God throughout my day with words of wisdom and words of knowledge and discerning of spirits and prophecy. It changed my life.

Pray for the purposes of God to be released and fulfilled. Pray for divine connections. Pray it in tongues. This is a prayer strategy that will help you build yourself up in the strongest way possible – direct communion with the Holy Spirit.

Stir up the Gifts

Stir up the gifts of the Holy Spirit within you. I mean literally lay hands on yourself and pray out loud:
" In the name of Jesus, I stir the gift of faith, the gift of working of miracles, the gifts of healing; I stir the gift of prophecy, tongues and interpretation of tongues; I stir the gifts of word of wisdom, word of knowledge and discerning of spirits. I stir the gift of serving, giving, leadership, teaching, preaching, mercy."

Literally pray it over yourself. You may focus on one area more than others, but do it knowing that as you stir up the gifts within you, praying in English and praying in tongues, you are building yourself up spiritually. (2 Timothy 1: 6) You will be so refreshed and so quickened by the Holy Spirit, you may want to go out and Evangelize immediately. Offer yourself to God and ask Him to use you so that you may use the gifts of the Spirit to help others.

Your Prayer Life

As you are praying for yourself, start praying for others as well. If you are a Christian, you will want to pray for others because you know God answers prayer. Sometimes, people ask us to pray for them and we casually say yes or meaningfully say yes but don't write it down and forget about it. It's best to take a moment and pray for that person right on the spot.; If the Holy Spirit impresses you, write it down and keep it on your prayer list. You may pray for something only once. You may pray for a situation repeatedly until you receive the answer.

If you do not have a prayer list, create one. Write all the points you want to pray about yourself. Write down others to pray about such as family and friends, your pastors, your church, other ministries etc. Keeping a list helps us to keep organized. You can diverge from your list but it is there as a reminder to help you, a guideline that you can constantly add to or change as desired.

Pray for Yourself the Scriptures

If you have not yet discovered this precious treasure, start doing it today. Start praying the scriptures for yourself. Find scriptures that have to do with things you are believing God for. Find scriptures with character qualities you want in your life; find scriptures that include promises etc. Pray scriptures over yourself and for others. Praying God's Word is special because it is His known will to us. Literally personalize the scripture. Don't just read it. There is a place for reading and confessing the scriptures but that is not what I am talking about here.

Example

Psalm 91

1 He who dwells in the shelter of the Most High
shall abide under the shadow of the Almighty.
2 I will say of the Lord, "He is my refuge and my fortress,
my God in whom I trust."

Pray out loud " Thank you God that I dwell in the secret place of the Most High. Thank you I live in the shadow of the almighty. Thank you. You, are my rock and my fortress. Thank you, You are my God that I trust."

I mean pray it and personalize it claiming the blessings of that word for your life as though it was written especially to you. If you don't read the Bible that way, I want to encourage you to start reading God's Word as though it directly written to you. God gave us His Word so we would have history of the Church and human origin; God gave us the Word to encourage us through Biblical stories – but Oh, if you do not know that the Word of God is a literal love letter to you expressing His will for you and all people, please start reading and praying your Bible that way.

Pray for God to release labourers into the harvest fields of the earth (Luke 10: 2). Pray that all the people groups of the earth come to know

Christ. It is so important that Jesus made it as a prayer request for us to follow. The only way that is going to happen is if people pray for a release of labourers and also obey the word and share Christ with local and global evangelism. Support ministries that go. If you are not active in global missions, help send others by giving finances to people who go to other nations preaching, serving, giving etc. There are thousands of reputable ministries that help people. Prayerfully consider who you should partner with. If their ministry has encouraged you spiritually, it's a natural fit – you should support them financially. The added bonus is that you are giving to global missions – a commandment of the LORD.

It is good to pray with others as well, but what I am talking about here is sowing to your own self in the Spirit. It is what you should do to invest in your spirit to strengthen and build your faith.

As you are giving to other ministries and praying for them, offer yourself and say Lord send me. If God presents you with the opportunity to preach, say yes.

Romans 12:1 I urge you therefore, brothers, by the mercies of God, that you present your bodies as a living sacrifice, holy, and acceptable to God, which is your reasonable service of worship.

I mean literally do it. I would include taking communion. Get the bread and the wine or juice. Kneel or sit and as you take the communion, thanking Jesus for giving His life for us, offer yourself to God. The Old Covenant includes offerings for sin – animals that were slain and their blood offered on our behalf. The most awesome thing we can offer to God in the New Covenant, is our lives – wholly: spirit soul and body each day, all the days of our lives.

Bible Study

Reading the Word of God in a disciplined manner is important. It can be a Bible study you purchase and follow or a Bible study that grows from your interest in certain areas of the Word. Yes, there are good Bible studies as a group, I'm not talking about them here. I am talking about your own self studying God's Word to strengthen yourself.

Bible For A Year

I don't see this Bible advertised as much as it once was, but it is an excellent way to read the Bible. It chunks the Bible into daily readings of

Old Testament, Psalms and Provers and New Testament. By reading it in daily chunks of about 15 minutes a day, within a year, you completely read through the Bible. It's an excellent method of covering as much scripture as possible into portions that are interesting and manageable. It is a pattern for reading the Bible through in a year. Keeping the Word of God refreshed in your spirit encourages you and aligns you with God. Also, should you be sharing Christ with someone or encouraging someone, the scriptures will be quickened to you and you will be able to sow them into people's lives. God's word never returns without impacting a life.

The Psalms and Proverbs are special and very important. The Psalms were written by worshippers who loved God and lived through all kinds of situations. They express love and worship of God whether things are prosperous, or whether they are fighting enemies. It would be good to learn these Psalms so they would be words we could confess and impart to others. The Proverbs are important because they give us the Old Testament version of tweets. There are mini verses that are packed with gems and treasure. Should God quicken them to you, they will transform your life.

You can ask the LORD what book of the Bible to start reading and studying, but if you do not hear a Word telling you which one, start reading and invite God to help you. I'm saying, sometimes God directs us specifically to certain books of the Bible or topics of study. Other times, you jump in and start reading and ask The Holy Spirit for Revelation. The Bible is God's Word. There have been occasions where the Lord has directed me to certain passages of scripture, but most of my Bible reading and study has come from me starting and inviting the Holy Spirit to guide me, teach me and give me revelation. The most important thing is get the Word of God inside of you. Pray about it. Receive it.

I would describe it as a chewing. I mean you take a portion and meditate on it and a new portion comes up and you take it and mediate on it and pray for revelation and insight. It keeps on chewing and coming up in your spirit as important – as a cow would chew its cud. It's kind of' gross but it is so true. As it comes up to importance in you, you meditate on it, digest it and pray for revelation. Next a different portion comes up and the pattern is repeated. We need to study the Word of God – not only read it but meditate on it and pray about it. Prayerfully read the Word of God.

The Best Bible Translation

There are so many translations of God's Word. Read the translation you can best understand. This book mostly uses the Modern English version (MEV edition); very popular is the NIV translation. I like the King James Version and prefer it. The Amplified Bible gives you the literal meaning of the words. It's usually a teacher's favourite Bible to use to show the meaning of the scriptures. The Internet has websites such as Bible Gateway that has over 25 versions in English and others in different other languages. The best edition of the Bible is the one you feel most comfortable with. It is the version that makes sense to you and you enjoy reading. I would recommend buying a physical copy of the Bible not instead of the digital versions but in addition to them. A paper copy you can underline in and write notes in is valuable. You learn from it not only as you read it but as you reread it.

Make it a point to study parts of your Bible. Read through the Bible for instance on angels or on good kings or on prophets. You can find scriptures on these topics and learn all you can as you read the scriptures concerning them. This message is for you if you want to learn all you can about God. This message is for you if you want to grow spiritually.

More of God

Bible study, prayer and building up yourself spiritually should be the most important aspects of your life. If you are single, you can freely do these things. It will mean less leisure activities but it will mean you can be strong and mighty for God. This message is directed to you who want all of God you can get. I remember myself, years ago, newly saved, crying out at the altar for all of God that God would give me. I meant it with all my being. I wanted as much as He would give. He has never said it is enough. The more I know Him, the more I want to know Him; the more I am fascinated by His character, the more He shows Himself in manifold ways. There is always more of God. He is completely beautiful and mighty, Holy and magnificent. There is always more. Throughout eternity we will be learning about God.

Get into a group Bible study with Christians

I have been so blessed by the excellence of ministry I have received. Once I became a Christian, I enrolled in a nine month Bible study on the whole Bible. It covered God's dealings with man from the Garden of Eden to the present day. It was packed with scriptures. I was rooted in the foundations of the faith because of this Bible study. The thing was I went to a mega church. There were Bible studies like a smorgasbord to choose from. For three years, I studied the doctrines of our faith and God's dealings with people. Afterwards I studied teacher's training and other mature adult Bible studies. It was awesome. If you have ever been to a buffet of only the best most awesome delicacies, that is exactly what I had the choice of. There was a choice of approximately 20 or more adult Bible classes on all sorts of topics. I would have liked to continue taking classes the rest of my life, but I knew God also wanted me to teach. It was tough on me because I wanted as much Word as I could get, but I began to teach Bible studies to children.

Please know that if two or more Christians get together to study the Bible, some sharpening of iron is going to take place. If the Christians are there in agreement studying God's Word, there will be revelation and insight. Whether you go to a large church such as I described, or a small church, get yourself into a Bible study with believers. It is a good way to build yourself up and also encourage others. This doesn't replace personal Bible study. It does though add excellence to your experience as a Christian. You will make godly Christian friends that way. You will be building up others and they will be building you up (Proverbs 27: 17).

Teaching

We in North America are so privileged to receive much teaching of God's Word. There are ministers not only in our local churches but some of the most excellent teaching and preaching is on the TV or on Satellite or on Cable or on the Internet. Often Christian Media was my spiritual family because I was the first Christian in my family. There is Christian music, entertainment, documentaries etc. But what I am talking about is supplementing your sermons with excellence of worldwide ministry preaching and teaching on faith, Bible Study, Giving, etc. Often, I would turn on the radio or TV to get totally encouraged by Christian preaching. Some of the people so encouraged me and feed me that I became partners with them financially as well as prayerfully. Others I gave a one-time gift, some I only pray for. I wish I could say that I prayed a blessing on every Christian minister who ever blessed me but it isn't true. I didn't understand how special a gift I had been given.

Sow the Word of God into your life. There are major Christian Networks in North America such as Trinity Broadcasting Network, Daystar, GODTV, and others. You may have local Christian stations. We do in my region. Watch Christian ministry or listen to it to build up your faith. What is awesome about these different Christian Networks that I have named is that they broadcast a wide variety of excellence from all over North America and often from Israel as well. You will get the best teaching and preaching in the comfort of your home. This is most certainly a way to build up and encourage yourself in God.

Friendships

As you press in to God, you will be with others who are doing the same thing. As you go the extra bit to get the Word of God in Bible study or in prayer etc. there will be certain people who will become your friends. They will be people who believe the same as you. They will be people who want the same things as you. These people who have the same priorities for more of God will bless you, strengthen you and refresh you. They will pray for you and pray with you. They will speak encouraging words to you and they may be of all different ages. Most of my closest friends during that period of my life were much older than me. They were mature Christians who invested in my life and complimented me by their association with me. These people were radical Christians. I learned from them to write scriptures on index cards and carry them throughout my day so I could look at them and pray them. I learned to put scriptures in the car over the visor so I could see it, pray it and believe it. I saw their true passion for God's Word and it encouraged me to press into God more myself.

Get in Prayer Meetings

If you do not go to a prayer meeting, I want to highly recommend that you join one or start one. I would attend all the prayer opportunities our Church offered. If I didn't have a job, I always attended the senior's meeting. Oh there were saints in that meeting who prayed, praised, danced and shouted. They would pray over me for a job and within a week or two I had a job. The only regret is that I was no longer able to get to their meeting. Prayer with seasoned saints teaches you things you might not learn any other way. Being together with corporate prayer is an awesome joy. You join your faith with others to see miracles manifest. I remember attending several different kind of prayer meetings and also in special situations, starting my own in my home with people who shared the same desire to pray for people or situations.

There were several prayer assignments in my life. I knew that I knew God placed these things on my heart to pray about and there were others who felt the same. We met and prayed every day until the answer manifested. It was radical. I knew and they knew God had called us to pray through for people's healing, revival etc. We lived much as the Apostles of the Book of Acts as we shared food together, prayed and praised and rejoiced once the miracles were manifest. It was the richest, most rewarding type of friendship I have even known. It is because it was God's idea and we came into agreement with God. Once the miracle manifested, we no longer gathered the same way. I thank God for those special meetings. The gifts of the Spirit were manifest and the Holy Spirit would often give a Word of prophesy or wisdom or discernment or a vision etc.

Matthew 18: 19 "Again I say to you, that if two of you agree on earth about anything they ask, it will be done for them by My Father who is in heaven. 20 For where two or three are assembled in My name, there I am in their midst."

The High Call of God

There is a call of God on every Christian's life. I don't mean all are called into the fivefold ministry of Apostle, Prophet, Pastor, Teacher, and Evangelist. We are all called to be ministers of reconciliation. We are all called to share Christ with others. God has a place for you that is a secret place that only You and God can enter in. It is a place of communion with God. Should you be single, you should be giving all your efforts towards the high call of God in Christ for your life. It will means prayer, Bible study, devotion etc. It is possible, you may meet your spouse by your faith filled living. It is possible, you may find your career by pressing in to God in this special way. Those who are married should also seek the high call of God but they must care about their spouse as a priority. That means if you are married, you must keep up your home and your cooking, cleaning, care for your husband or wife. If there are children, God wants you to care for them. You must honour your spouse and your family and cannot neglect them in any way. This would be direct disobedience to God.

Single, Teenagers, Widowed, Divorced

It is easier for a single person to devote his or her life towards God. Please know, some are called into the fivefold ministry and God may reveal it to you. Also, you may be wholly devoting yourself to God and find a spouse or career. This special place of seeking God with all your being may be in your life in your teens or 20's or 30's. It may be with you all your life. Some widowed or divorced person's may enter this place I'm talking about. It doesn't mean you will be able to give yourself wholly in the same way all of your life. As long as you are single, in your teens or 20's or 30's – press into God with all you have got to get His best for you. God can use your passion to lead others to Christ, to build His Church and to release giftings and callings in your own life.

Your pressing into God seeking His best for your life, will never be wasted. Your giving of your whole self to God may lead you into divine connections with people. It may help you find your place of ministry in the Church. It may confirm to you your plans for education and career. Please know your efforts of pressing in to God are never wasted. If you are able to press in – press in all you can. Candidates are usually single, teens or 20's or 30's or divorced or widowed or alone for some reason.

Rather than be passive and allow life to pass you by, take hold of yourself and set your sight on God. Focus on God more than anything else. Fix your eyes on Jesus and His beauty (Hebrews 12: 2). Set your heart to praise and to worship God and to learn all you can about God. I tell you surely you will be living in joy and peace and fellowship with others of like precious faith. Most certainly if you remained in this place all your life you would never lack or be without joy. The truth is though, it is often a trampoline of faith that leads you into specific directions that God will make clear to you. What you will have though is an awesome intimacy with God than will never be lost. You will never regret pressing in to God if you are doing it for the motive of wanting to know Him.

4 THE HIGH CALLING OF GOD IN CHRIST JESUS

You decide how much of God you want. Do you want the high calling of God in Christ Jesus for your life? There is a way above the ways of the earth even though God wants to use you on the earth. It is a way of Holiness. It is the way of the Spirit. Don't believe the lie that anything in your past can stop God from using you. Thank Jesus for His blood regularly. Confess His righteousness alone is your righteousness. As you press in for more of God, the anointing on your life becomes stronger. You will want to serve, to give, to participate in things for God. You will develop special love for God's people and for all people. I would add special love for all creatures but that may be only specific to me – I care about all life forms.

The High Calling

The high calling is being one with God throughout your daily life. It is total consecration. You literally pray giving yourself to God. You ask God to use you. What happens? God uses you. He responds by anointing you and positioning you into places where God can use you. Some it may seem really ordinary but because God is using you it has spiritual significance. God has a high calling for all of us but in order to live it you have a part to play. You must be willing; you must be obedient; you must pursue God continuously. That was what God was thinking as you became a thought; He thought of the best you could possibly be – He thought of you participating in labour with Him. The Holy Spirit wants to be the Senior partner of your life. In business, the Senior partner has more authority; the senior partner has more influence; the senior partner often wins contracts or negotiations based on reputation. God wants to prompt you and lead you as you go throughout your normal life – using you in special ways to affect people on the earth.

God created you for His glory. You using your gifts and talents, education and training, family, friends, relationships etc. (all that is particular to your life) to its fullest maximum capacity is what God wants for you. You living your life pursuing God, willing and obedient, participating with the Holy Spirit will be completely satisfied and even overflowing with thankfulness. You will begin to see opportunities for you to share and give and care. No matter what may occur, should you be living this way of Spirit, some authors call it the sweet spot, the most rewarding and fulfilling life possible will be yours. It will seem like heaven on earth. It doesn't mean there may not be difficulties or obstacles. Your faithful pressing into God will make it smooth and hopeful. God's plan for all people is that they should have the best life possible. Some Christians who know they are saved, who are baptized in the Holy Spirit, do not pursue God further and are not living in their high calling.

You can live a lukewarm life as a Christian who attends church, reads a devotional or the Bible, lives the rest of his or her life simply being there. It is comfortable. Someone else is always serving. Someone else is always giving. Someone else is always preaching or encouraging. Others are always the main participants. The Christian not living in his or her high call will simply absorb and absorb and absorb as though being waited on. They will never consider offer themselves to God for God to use them. They will never obey the promptings of the Spirit. They can live a mediocre Christian existence. Please know that is not the way God made it to be. Do a self-evaluation here.

If praise and worship seems boring,
If you don't desire God first
If you don't want to be used by God
If you don't want to apply God's Word to your life and to others
If you don't care about the church

You should decide why you are a Christian. God is not boring. He is fascinating. If you are really a Christian, you will want to be in His presence and share His truth by preaching and teaching Christ in the earth. You will want to serve God not because you must but because it is your delight. Never believe the lie that Christian life is boring. God is fascinating and relationship with Him is exciting. God who created all things wants to commune with us - mere humans. Jesus died to raise us up so we could sit together with Him in heavenly places in Christ. Jesus gives us opportunity to be a partner with Him in our lives. What would your life be like if you let God use you? It would be the most awesome exciting life you could ever have on earth.

Psalm 139: 13 You brought my inner parts into being;
    You wove me in my mother's womb.

God chose you, your gifts, talents, desires, characteristics, and placed you in your mother's womb. It was a delicate, deliberate weaving together of all aspects of your personality, with your body features, your parents and earthy family etc. Many Christians will agree with me on these points, but please see that isn't the end of the Divine plan. Your getting saved isn't the end of the Divine plan. It's awesome that you are saved. It's awesome you were filled with the baptism of the Holy Spirit speaking in other tongues. That is only for your equipping. That is only the start of what God wants to do in your life. God wants to use you in the spheres of influence of your life.

Spheres of Authority

Loren Cunningham and Bill Bright (1995) from Youth with a Mission and Campus Crusade listed 7 spheres of society that people can influence.

Family
Education
Entertainment
Economy, Business
Entertainment
Religion
Government

I would add in one extra that I believe is an important sphere and it is health care and technology. I believe there is such a huge impact in these fields that it should be listed as separate. Each person has influence in some of these fields. Some fields are more predominant than others to different people depending on their education, skills and training and career choices, marital status etc. You are in some of these spheres now. Determine within yourself you want to impact these spheres. You want to make a difference by your giving and serving and living as a Christian in these spheres.

I won't go into detail in this book, but please start praying over your areas of influence. Examine your spheres of influence. What are they? Don't say none. If you are a student, you are in the sphere of education. You don't have the same authority as your teacher but you have influence with your peers, your teachers etc. all within that sphere.

1.   Determine your spheres of influence, first. I would write them in a journal or a special place, so that you could examine them and re-examine them prayerfully. Your spheres change as your life changes.

2.   Determine how can you best add value to the people in your spheres of influence. Consider how you can you improve life in the community you live in. You can make a difference. You may not believe this because you may be a teen ager or believe yourself to be insignificant. It's not true. God

can use you at any age to make a difference in your spheres of influence.

3.   Believe that God can use you to make a difference.

It has to do with attitude. Know that since God saved you, since God revealed His mercy to you, He wants to use you. Give yourself willingly and with obedience and be proactive. Start each day with a desire to help someone or to give your best or to serve with excellence or to listen and give wise advice. Whatever your everyday normal life seems like, you can be on the lookout for opportunities for God to use you. Watch for opportunities that you can use to give God your best.

As a normal student, you are in spheres of family, education, business, entertainment and religion. Begin to think of how you could contribute. God can give you an idea for your class to raise money for the food bank It can be an idea for your school to sponsor a refugee family to come to your country. Begin assessing what the needs are of the area of your life. Pray for solutions. God can give you an idea to radically transform someone's life. God can use a student in student government in a school to encourage the whole school and bring them together for a good cause that will also build up the school spirit and encourage all the students to give their best. Please see, you can make a difference. Find the ways that you can and begin doing something. First should be prayer.

There are things to pray about. There are also things to do to take action. For instance, a student a school has no food for lunch repeatedly. You notice it. You don't have to pray. Share your lunch with that student. If there are a number of students who have no lunch, pray and approach a teacher and the principal to do something about it. I have taught in schools where this is very much the case. The students are so poor and their living condition such that they get no breakfast or lunch. The schools adopted breakfast programs for the kids and other schools, a kid will bring two lunches – one for himself and one to share.

Everyday Life

Usually, you go about your life doing whatever you should as a student or professional. If you see a need you can obviously meet, do something about it. If it is bigger than you, get help. Part of that help would be prayer and asking God to lead you to the right people. Mostly God uses us in ordinary ways to be a blessing to people. Our serving, giving, loving, encouraging etc. is what makes it special. There are special opportunities where God may use you such as the examples I have given you. Both service to God as a faithful citizen of your country and faithful willingness and obedience to God are important ways to serve on the earth. Pray about your spheres of influence and always pray for Divine connections so that God can put people who can be a blessing to you in your life and so that God can place people in your life who you can be a blessing to.

Knit within your spirit are desires, likes, wants, things that are appealing to you, things you want. These very things that make you unique were placed there by God who gave them to you. Please know I am talking about things such as wanting to help people, wanting to start a business, wanting to play sports etc. These talents, aptitudes and gifts help define you and set you apart from others. Never believe the lie that your life is not important. God cared so much for you that He wove you together and placed you in your mother's womb. It's God who wanted you, so even if people tell you horrible things such as your life doesn't matter, know that it matters to God. God has a purpose for your life. Whether or not your earthly family knows it, you are a gift of God to the earth and to them. Your talents and gifts can be used to impact the earth and spheres of influence you are a part of. These things you are good at and enjoy doing, your strengths are part of the high calling of God for you. Using them gives your spheres of opportunity to meet people and to be a witness for Christ.

The very things that give you pleasure such as playing baseball or soccer or playing an instrument or dancing, all of these things God can use for His glory. These things placed inside of you before your birth, how important it is so important that you pray over your own child as it is in the womb. It is so important is it that you pray for your own children to use their gifts and talents for Christ that God entrusted you with their lives. Start praying for your children's life before it is born. Pray for friends, for talents, for a career – you can be prayerfully confessing scriptures over your child. Start positive Christian parenting as soon as you know of the pregnancy.

Parents should encourage and help their children develop these gifts and talents but not all people have parents who can do it. Some people are in single parent homes; some people have less than ideal family situations. In spite of all these things that could hinder you, I am saying God can make a way for you to accomplish much and to develop, use your gifts and talents. It is possible to achieve your dreams. We who live in the western World, free society have some many freedoms that we take for granted. Please see here in North America, nothing can stop you from going to school. We have loans and grants to help us get to school. Even if you have to pay back the student loans for many years, do it; get all the education you can get. I can tell you that I would not have the excellent job I presently have if it had not been for those loans and bursaries. Education is important in our society. It opens opportunities for us to careers that are rewarding and fulfilling.

Psalm 139: 14 I will praise you, for You made me with fear and wonder;
    marvelous are Your works,
    and You know me completely

God Can Use You

God breathed life into the body of Adam that he formed from the earth. He is the same God who gave you all aspects of your being and placed in in your mother's womb. God could use you because He created you for His glory. God could use you because you gave your life to Him. God can use you because you are willing and obedient. God can use you because that was Hid purpose in creating you: that you would have relationship with Him and that He could share your life by leading and guiding you.

You Can Sow Into Yourself

You should do all you can to develop your talents and gifts. Should you be a teenager or twenty or thirty something, you will know the things that you always wanted to do but perhaps your parents didn't encourage you in for whatever reason. It is less than what is ideal but that doesn't mean you must stay there. Usually, most high schools have music as an option to take as a class. You can learn an instrument. You can get involved in your school. You can get a part time job and take music lessons or art classes or dance or join a sports team. You can invest in yourself. You can do those things you always wanted to do.

If you do not do all you can to develop your gift or talent, you are not being a wise steward of what God has given to you and you will be accountable to God to answer for it. Your gift is never only for you; it is for you to share with others. First, while you are learning the skill or instrument, you are making friends and learning the important aspects. It will give you joy as you use the gift or talent. It will bring people you know and that care about you to watch you perform. It will be a connection point of celebration for them.

I have known of some Christians who had talent on the piano and taught themselves to play it. Some of them became worship leaders. I have known of others who did not get the teaching but they would dance and sing and bang their tambourines in church worshipping God with all their might. They gave what they could. The spiritual anointing on someone who is using his or her gift or talent can be so strong that it literally influences the spiritual atmosphere. It can activate faith in the atmosphere so people could be saved or healed or receive some other miracle of God. Using your gifts in the Church can release others to use their gifts. Just as God placed all parts of your body soul and spirit together, God placed you in a local church. You are part of the Spiritual Body of Christ. Your gifts and talents affect those around you and vice versa.

Psalm 139: 14 and You know me completely.

God knew you completely before you were born. He knew your potential. He knew what you could be, what you could do. You do not have to agree with God but it would be foolish not to. God gave you the talents, the gifts, the desires, the opportunities; all you must do is come into agreement with Him. You do all you can to develop your gifts and talents and give your best effort in all that you do. You get all the education and training you can get. You offer yourself to God wholly expecting God to use you. Yes. It involves work on your part; you have to give your best; you have to develop your talents, you have to give God your all – but what a blessing you will receive should you give your life to God. Your will never be fully satisfied any other way. God wants you to shine as a bright star at your full potential. It gives you prosperity and happiness; it gives God glory and pleasure.

Servants Wanted

There is a need in the church for servants – those who will serve God by doing practical things such as clean, wash cars, volunteer to teach Sunday school, serve food to people etc. If you are young and able, God can use you to serve in your church in this capacity. People who are married with children have a schedule that makes it harder for them to make such commitments. People that are older may also serve in the church, but I am emphasizing to you that God may use you to be a vital part of the Hands of God in the Church today – by serving. What it will do is connect you with other Christians who enjoy doing the same kinds of things. You will make friends with people. You will begin to learn areas of the church you enjoy serving in and may stay in that role most of your church life.

Sure Opportunities For Serving: Within your Church and Community

Caring for the Single Parents

Your willingness to serve in church frees other leaders such as the pastors to do other things. If you know you enjoy serving and you know God has used you in serving, let me express to you a real need in most every local church. There are some single mums who perhaps need someone to care for their children while they do chores. Perhaps you could mow the lawn for them or shovel snow. You would be directly helping someone in need. Some single parents cannot get to church because of their children's schedules your volunteering there can make a big impact. You can free that mum to get some of the word of God to refresh her spirit. You can be a teacher of those children and show the love of God towards them.

You could help an elderly man or woman do chores around his or her home. You could learn from them spiritual things, while you help serve them in practical ways.

Caring for Single Parent Kids

Not all Christian kids have a big brother or big sister. You could make a difference by volunteering to befriend a kid and care for him or her as if for your own family. These kids might never get to play baseball if you don't invite them and take an interest in their lives. These kids might not ever get to see a symphony or concert play if you don't invite them.

Start searching for potential places where you can give your service. I know you are busy. I know you can't always do all things, but you can do something and while you are doing it you can be directly encouraging and building up others.

Sow into people's lives on purpose, expecting nothing except from the LORD. This is a direct way of serving. God would be using you to serve. It isn't glamorous but it is important. Your serving can make a tremendous difference in someone's life. You might not even consider this a ministry but it is. It requires some commitment on your part. You could give one hour or two to start. Most teens and twenty somethings could do it if they believed it was making a difference in people's lives.

Adopt the new Christians

If you know that a person is the first Christian in his or her family, invest in that person. Believe me it is all the difference in the world whether or not you do. I had some Bible teachers who invested in my life by inviting me into their home. After I was done the Bible class (nine month study), they asked me to stay in the class as a helper. I loved them and did. They entrusted to me positions of authority. They got me to help do things like sell tickets, or take attendance. Later they got me to pray publicly. It was hard for me but I did it because they believed in me. They got me involved in Nursing Home Ministry and special Bible class functions. They got me to lead worship. They treated me as if I were their own daughter. I so thank God for the, because I had no knowledge of any of these things. Their investment in my life helped me to see what a Christian family and Christian Lifestyle was truly about.

If you are teaching a Bible class, invest in some of the students. Train them up and show them how to use their gifts and talents. God will give you a special love for each other and you will be directly investing into their lives and into the kingdom of God. Even if you are a teen ager, you can encourage those your age or children; you can train them in things you've learned. Once you start giving to others in this way, you will always want to do more of it because it is enjoyable and you can see the fruit of it in the people's lives by seeing them use their gifts and talents and things you taught them.

Visitation

Visitation is not only for the pastors. You could arrange to visit shut ins. You could bring your instrument and go to visit shut ins and sing and perform for them. Your showing up, could release joy in them. You could read scripture to a person or share a brief testimony. Your visit may be the only one that person has seen for a week.

Connecting People

This usually involves serving and encouragement. The ability to connect people for purposes of enjoyment is a gift. You invite people for a dinner or movie or concert. This is a form of leadership gift expressed. People who might never meet each other any other way get together because of you. You can invite someone to your home or out for lunch. If you notice a new person at church, you could connect over coffee. Being friendly is an aspect of the gift of encouragement. I have known people who could invite all different kinds of people to an event such as a movie or a concert or a party. People will meet others who they don't normally meet. It is a tremendous way to serve in the church. If you are able, you can invite them to your home. Once you have your own place, certainly you can invite people.

I had no Christians in my family. People from my church invited me to events and to their home for dinner and Christian conversation. I can tell you if they didn't invite me I wouldn't have known what it was because I didn't get it any place else. I thank God for those who showed me such welcoming and some adopted me as family and included me in family events and activities. God put it on their hearts to care for me. I thank God for them.

I wanted to invite others to my home but was ashamed of the home. I lived in a very small, plain cold in the winter, hot in the summer home; it needed much repair and was unappealing. I made many sacrifices to attend post-secondary school and didn't have the money to improve the home. I didn't like to invite people to my home unless I knew them really well. I was good at connecting people though and would sometimes get someone who had a larger home that was pleasing, to host an event such as a Bible study or party. It brought me joy and brought joy to all that came. We helped in all ways possible to those who hosted the event to make it easy for them to clean up.

Volunteer

In Ontario, Canada, it is mandatory that all high school students do at least 40 hours of community service before they get their diploma. I believe this is an excellent policy because it gives the students job experience and experience with people to help prepare them for further jobs. You could choose to do any of these acts of serving that I am expressing. There is a sincere true need in most churches concerning these things. You could be getting volunteer credit for serving and be developing in your talents and gifts and blessing others while you do it.

Even if you live in a different province or a state does not require volunteer work, let me highly encourage you to do some because it gives you direct work experience you can place on your resume. People will view you as a motivated individual for serving. At minimum, you get work experience. It is possible, your experience at that place or for those people could turn to a paying job for you.

Investing and Mentoring

Should you be using your spiritual gifts, you should always try to draw others around you that you can train. Teachers, should you notice a child sensitive to the things of God, sow the Word of God into that person; encourage him or her to pursue God. Pastors, should you notice someone hanging on the edge of the seat in your Bible study, invite him or her to dinner. Invest some of yourself into that person's life encouraging him or her to press into Christ. Sharing your life's experience with others is more than just being in service together. God can give you special love for those you train. If each of us in the body of Christ duplicated ourselves – reproduction not only physical – I mean sow some of what was taught to you into others you see the gift in, so we would build up, strengthen and establish the Church as we should. Successful people, should be encouraging other people to pursue the high calling of God for their lives.

1 Corinthians 14: 26 How is it then, brothers? When you come together, every one of you has a psalm, a teaching, a tongue, a revelation, and an interpretation. Let all things be done for edification.

Encourage the People to use their Gifts

Prophesy, words of encouragement, exhortation and comfort should not be a rare occasion in our gathering together as a church. There should be tongues and interpretation of tongues and prophesy. These gifts are a sign of life in the church. The gifts of the Spirit flourish as we wait on God after praise and worship, also by encouraging those who use their gifts. Also, by thanking God for the gifts. As we gather together, the Spirit of God will quicken someone to read a scripture, someone to speak in tongues, someone to prophesy, someone to bring a song.

The moving of the Holy Spirit through the body with the evidence of Spiritual gifts manifest is something to thank God for and to encourage. We want our children to hear prophesy and tongues in the church so that when he or she gets a prompting in the spirit, he or she will understand what to do. Those who were not raised as Christians, learn about the things of the Spirit by being in the sanctuary and in communion with other Christians.

The gift of encouragement is not only for the pastors and the greeters in the church. If you attend church and someone's prophetic word encouraged you, speak it to that person. Thank him or her for sharing the Word. If you received a blessing from the praise and worship, thank that person for using his or her gift for the LORD. Kind words of appreciation that are true and sincere make a difference. It shows the Body building up and encouraging the body. It means all the body will be strengthened. Greeters in the church should be smiling, friendly and spiritual. They are usually the first people someone sees coming into church. The anointing of God should be upon them for encouragement. As they shake hands and welcome people, they should literally believe they are imparting a welcoming blessing of peace and grace to the person. It is a ministry – greeting people.

Those who serve in any capacity in the church should pray asking for Christ to shine through them so others would want to know Jesus and they could speak things that would strengthen and encourage those you see. Should all people serving in the Church realize that body ministry is essential, God may quicken scriptures to them. God may use your words to touch someone's heart giving them a special glimpse of God through your kindness.

Hebrews 4: 12 For the word of God is alive, and active, and sharper than any two-edged sword, piercing even to the division of soul and spirit, of joints and marrow, and able to judge the thoughts and intents of the heart.

Isaiah 55: 11 so shall My word be that goes forth from My mouth; it shall not return to Me void, but it shall accomplish that which I please,

There are natural duties that must be done in a local church such as running the sound and lighting, being ushers, being greeters, running all forms of media, serving coffee etc. There Are also supernatural opportunities that come to those who serve in any of these or other capacities; it is because should you be willing and obedient and prayerful thank God for what you are contributing, God can shine through you with special excellence and anointing. The anointing is a special grace of God's presence on you that attracts people to God.

Colossians 3: 23 And whatever you do, do it heartily, as for the Lord and not for men, 24 knowing that from the Lord you will receive the reward of the inheritance. For you serve the Lord Christ.

Encouragers Make a Difference

God wants to use all the members of the local church to shine God's glory. Some are ministers, some are leaders, some are servants, some are choir members; some are musicians etc. Each part is vital and God can use you to show the light of God's love to the people gathered. Those newly saved should be given opportunities to help serve in some capacity because they are usually so exuberant for God they can barely contain it. They show passion and zeal for God in anything they do. They could be trained to be greeters and to be ushers, to serve and with kitchen duties. The pastors and leaders should learn who the encouragers are in the church so they can appoint them different places throughout all the church service areas.

Should you attend a church newly saved, you are not a mature Christian after year one. Yes you have learned much; yes there is still much you can learn. Press into others who show similar gifting to your own. If you are serving in the church, initiate conversation with other servants. If you are an usher, make friends with other ushers. If you are passionate about Bible study, press in; invite your pastor or teacher for coffee. I go to a large church so it isn't always possible to go for a coffee with the main pastor but there are other leaders; press in and invite one of them. Learn all you can from those God gives you opportunity to learn from. It might mean you have to start a conversation or ask for a meeting. Normally it occurs by Divine appointment. The things you love and gravitate to in the church, God uses them to place the right people around you who will take you under their wing and teach you and encourage you. You will be a blessing to them and they will be a blessing to you.

Keep an open dialogue with your leaders. If you can't see them face to face, email them or write them. If they are being led by the Holy Spirit, they will invite you to join them in some way to strengthen you.

Megachurches

The advantage to going to a mega church or a large church is that something is going on every day in the church. I mean there are different prayer meetings, volleyball, women's meetings, men's meetings, sports, teenage classes, foundations of the faith teaching, mature Christian Bible studies etc. Not all people are expected to go to all meetings. There is something for everyone. This is a major positive aspect of a large church.

Small churches don't have to be left behind in terms of opportunities and training. The pastors need support by elders and deacons and mature Christians who would teach a Bible study or mentor a new Christian. The pastor of a small church should not be expected to do it all. People in the congregation need to own the ministry of the church also, realizing their contributions matter. Someone can teach kids praise dancing; someone can have a special teen Bible study. The pastors of such a church would truly be able to minister with liberty if everyone in the church were taking a part.

Givers

Giving the tithe or first 10% of your income is taught to us clearly in the scriptures. God promises to financially bless you in your job and career should you be a tither.

Malachi 3: 10 Bring all the tithes into the storehouse, that there may be food in My house, and test Me now in this, says the Lord of Hosts, if I will not open for you the windows of heaven and pour out for you a blessing, that there will not be room enough to receive it.

There are different types of giving in the Church above the tithe. There is offerings which may be general to be used as needed or special offerings for the church building or needs of the church. There are alms that we give to help the poor and those who have need. There is a first fruits offering which is finances to thank God for blessing you in your increase in finances. Should you get a raise, you give a gift of first fruits giving of the extra money you made. First fruits giving is completely a free will offering. If you want to thank God for blessing you with a good job, you give a special offering.

Be a Giver

Let me encourage you to be a giver in different ways. If you have the finances and the opportunity, you could buy Christian books or materials for those who couldn't afford it. You could sow into others' lives. At one point in my life I was without a job and it was pretty financially tough for me.

A sister in Christ, who only knew me from Sunday gatherings, knew the importance of giving because she always spoke with me as though I mattered to her. One Sunday she gave me a cheque that was more money than I had seen in a while. I thanked God for her. She knew I had a specific need and sowed financially into my life. She didn't have to do that. It caused me to thank God and to learn that I should care about those I may only see in the sanctuary. She was the type of person, so gentle and so Christ like. She always came with her mother. She invited me to celebrate thanksgiving with them as a family. It was such a blessing to me. It mattered significantly to my life. She was not a leader in the church but she was a leader in giving and showing the love of Christ to new Christians. She did it by the leading of the Holy Spirit.

Should you have a bit of extra cash, invite someone for coffee or for lunch. You could be significantly improving his or her life by your generosity. It is a small thing but its impact can be huge. It is not only for the Pastors to notice the needs in the congregation. If you know someone has no food, give some money to the person or inform the pastor. If you notice a need that is important, you should tell the pastor. Example, once a nice elderly lady (she was in her 90's) who always sat near me stopped coming to church. I spoke to her family member and found out about it. I brought a friend and we went to visit her and pray with her. I wrote a brief note to the pastor knowing that because it was a large church, he didn't know about her situation. He made a special visit to see her and it encouraged her so much. Your caring about others who sit around you matters. Yes. Givers can be taken advantage of, but we should pray for discernment. Should I find out that a person scammed me, it would bother me; what would bother me more is if I found out the person had a real need and I didn't give; I didn't help but I could have.

Spiritual Discernment

I always encourage people who are newly saved to pray for spiritual discernment. Even after many years of being saved, I pray for spiritual discernment regularly. It is only by the Spirit of God I know what to do in certain situations. Spiritual discernment is necessary for any ministry in the church and for all members of the body of Christ. Being led by the Spirit of God, and having discernment and wisdom are important for all Christians. The Holy Spirit can lead you in using your gifts and prompt you to speak; the Holy Spirit can warn you; the Holy Spirit can give you wisdom beyond all earthly wisdom.

Leadership

We need leaders who will not only lead people but also train people to become leaders. By investing in someone, you can strengthen his or her gifts and talents and strengthen him or her to use those leadership gifts. All parent have to know how to be leaders in their families. All teens have to know how to be leaders in their classes at school and in their family and in the church. Invite some kids from school to your home for a party. Give some Christian word of evangelism of what Christ has done for you. You don't have to be long – but you must be sincere. Should you do it, you could be the connection of that kid to Christ. Pray about it. Your practical inclusion of your faith into your everyday life can make a difference.

5 ALL THE MEMBERS OF THE BODY OF CHRIST ARE IMPORTANT

1 Corinthians 12: 14 The body is not one part, but many.

Oh, I long to see the gifts of the Spirit flowing in the Church. All the people flowing in their gifts, giving their best as unto Christ. Servants, encouragers, givers, people in faith, prophesy etc.

The whole body is important – all the parts. Just as your little finger doesn't seem important; if you lose it you realize how important it is. All parts of your body are important. That includes rich and poor; that includes children, teens, adults, special needs people. If each part was functioning in his or her gift of the sprit, we would have explosions of the love of God in our midst. We would see the glory cloud of God on our congregations.

I have been in churches where some of the poorest people attend. I mean the person was so poor that he or she didn't smell clean. I mean that person had only one dress or one shirt and pants. I have also seen the body of Christ around that person respond. Several of the men who sat around that man that smelled, invested in him. They bought him several suits of clothes and I don't know what else they did, but he didn't smell anymore. It was easier to greet him and to talk with him because the smell had been repulsive. Parts of the body of Christ – the ones sitting around the person can make a difference. I don't believe the pastor even knew about it (it was a large church). Those parts that seem unimportant can with love and care be made to flourish and not only would his or her natural life improve, but he or she could realize the love of God more and be able to give testimony of what God has done for them though the members of the body.

It is important that we treat all people with dignity and respect realizing it could be us in that position of need. The body should care for all members of the body. That poor person, or person who cannot give as others for whatever disability or need, is a member of Christ on the earth – there to see what you will do with this person. Your love should not only be for the most popular people or the richest people. You may be able to reach some that your pastor may never reach because they sit in the back row and enter and exit quickly. You can show the love of Christ to that person.

A Testimony

I was a university student without much money, I had one skirt – I wore it every week to church; I was clean but I only had one. Those spiritual parents I mentioned earlier who trained me in teaching and ministry, cared for me; the woman (my friend and spiritual parent) invited me to her home and let me choose from a huge pile of extra clothes she had. We were about the same size. I got dresses and skirts and coats etc. I could never repay her. It made a difference to me in more than one way. It made me thankful. It made me realize that is what Christians do – they care for each other like family.

Ask God to use you and look for opportunities in the church. Pursue the high calling of God in Christ Jesus. Be more like Jesus. Serve; give; volunteer; care about the members of the body of Christ you can influence; care about those who do not yet know the LORD. Know your gifts and your talents; use them. Learn all you can from others who have similar giftings. Pursue those who are spiritual and can teach you; offer to mentor others around you. Be connected in the body of Christ realizing it is your Christian family. Ask God to cause you to love the Church the way He loves the Church. Choose the best for yourself – pursue God with all your being; teach others there is a best for them as well.

Prayer for you (As you read it come into agreement with me if you believe as I am praying).

I pray that God will quicken the gift of faith in you so that the scriptures will be mixed with faith and produce spiritual fruit in your life. I pray you will diligently seek God for the promises of God for your life, that you will hold onto the promises of God believing that He who promised is able to do what He said and that He is faithful to do it also.

May God will give you Divine connections, people who can mentor you and train you up in your gifts and callings with practical and valuable service within the church and to the Body of Christ.

I pray that you will offer yourself a willing, holy, living sacrifice to God (Romans 12: 1-2) so that you learn all you can. I pray that if you are a student, God will lead you in your studies and in your future career, that you will get as much education and training as possible so that you can be successful and prosperous in the earth.

May God use you as you serve in the Church, and give you spiritual discernment. That God will direct you to use your gifts and talents for His glory. May God cause you to see the talents and gifts in others so that you can encourage them and help to train them to be servants in the Church.

I pray your faith will remain strong. It is God's Word that makes you an overcomer. You are God's chosen son or daughter. He wants to prosper you financially, physically, socially, spiritually etc. God is a good God. I pray you will put your trust in Him and what He says about you in the Word of God, and you will experience the overwhelming joy of His Holy presence and His equipping you with the Spiritual gifts. May God cause you to recognize the potential in the provision of the people and resources He has given you in your life.

I pray you would come to know the spheres of society you can influence and that you will use all of your strength to be a light for Christ within your spheres of authority.

May God pour out upon you a spirit of prayer and praise and supplication and intercession. May God, make you a leader among your peers. May God, give you strength above all earthly strength.

Joshua 1: 9 Have not I commanded you? Be strong and courageous. Do not be afraid or dismayed, for the Lord your God is with you wherever you go.

Chris Legebow

PRAYERS

PRAYER of Rededication of Your Life to Jesus Christ

God, thank you for drawing me. I thank you Jesus that you died for me on the cross and rose from the dead, ascended into heaven. I thank you for the promise that you are returning one day as you promised you would.

I confess that I have sinned. I have not served you with all my heart, soul mind and strength. Jesus please forgive me. I thank you for your blood that washes all sin and iniquity from me. (1 John 1: 9) Because I confess my sin and I believe you died for me, you wash me from all sin and iniquity. I am made Holy by the righteousness of God through Jesus Christ.

Holy Spirit quicken me. Examine me. Show me what things I must change so that I can be wholly living for God each day of my life. Help me to see the importance of living my life in light of eternity.
Give me discernment strong so I will know what things are pleasing to you. I give myself to you a living sacrifice (Romans 12: 1-2). I ask you to live in me. Holy Spirit increase my capacity to receive from you.

Holy Spirit, I ask you to warn me or correct me if I do things not pleasing to you or listen or watch things that are not pleasing to you. I want to love what you love and hate what you hate.

O God, renew my first love for you – the joy of my salvation.

Give me divine connections, godly people who I can learn from and also minister to. Use me. I give you my life fresh today. O God thank you for hearing and answering my prayer. Amen.

If you are not Baptized in the Holy Spirit sample prayer:

"Thank you God that you promised believers could be baptized in the Holy Spirit with the evidence of speaking in other tongues. Jesus I worship you; I ask you to fill me to overflowing with the Holy Spirit. I thank you by faith; I receive the gift of God promised to believers in Jesus Christ, the baptism of the Holy Spirit. Amen."

The words don't have to be exact but you must pray in faith believing the gift of the Holy Spirit is for all believers in the LORD Jesus Christ, including yourself. Pray thanking God for saving you and for the things He has done for you. Thank God. Then start praising God. Begin to worship God with all your being – be open to receiving from the LORD. God will bring the words to you but you must cooperate by speaking them out loud. As the words come to you speak them. Keep a heart of thanksgiving and worship. God will give you a prayer language that you can and should use.

You can receive the Baptism of the Holy Spirit all by yourself. You cn also ask a believer who is baptized in the Holy spirit to pray for you.

After you are baptized in the Holy Spirit, begin to thank God for filling you; pray that God might reveal your spiritual gifts to you and to use you in them. May God bless you as you continue to press in closer to The LORD Jesus Christ.

OTHER BOOKS BY CHRIS LEGEBOW

Available on Amazon.ca Amazon.com or Amazon.ca or Kindle
Or the Create Space webstore.

Discovering and Using your Spiritual Gifts. Living Word. 2016.

Kinds of Prayer. Knowing Them and Using Them Effectively.: Living Word. 2016.

Living Life Fully: Knowing your Purpose. Living Word. 2016.

The High Calling: Life Worth Living. Living Word. 2016.

ABOUT THE AUTHOR

Chris Legebow is a Christian Professor of English and Communications. She has taught at the elementary, high school and College and University levels. She has ministered in her local churches in intercessory prayer, teaching Sunday school and other Christian Doctrine classes to children and youths. She has preached to congregations and given her testimony. Although she was not raised in a Christian home, she came to know Jesus Christ as her Saviour and LORD while she was studying in University. This radically transformed her life in terms of priorities and commitment.

She has a strong passion for the great commission – that Jesus Christ would be preached throughout all the earth believing that it a major sign of the LORD's return. She has been a part of several different types of full gospel charismatic churches but has also gained much of her insight and enlightenment from Christian Media and broadcasting. She hopes to continue ministering, serving, interceding and giving and teaching until the LORD returns.

www.ingramcontent.com/pod-product-compliance
Lightning Source LLC
Chambersburg PA
CBHW020514030426
42337CB00011B/384